CAMBRIDGE LIBRARY COLLECTION

Books of enduring scholarly value

Travel and Exploration

The history of travel writing dates back to the Bible, Caesar, the Vikings and the Crusaders, and its many themes include war, trade, science and recreation. Explorers from Columbus to Cook charted lands not previously visited by Western travellers, and were followed by merchants, missionaries, and colonists, who wrote accounts of their experiences. The development of steam power in the nineteenth century provided opportunities for increasing numbers of 'ordinary' people to travel further, more economically, and more safely, and resulted in great enthusiasm for travel writing among the reading public. Works included in this series range from first-hand descriptions of previously unrecorded places, to literary accounts of the strange habits of foreigners, to examples of the burgeoning numbers of guidebooks produced to satisfy the needs of a new kind of traveller - the tourist.

Memoirs of the Chief Incidents of the Public Life of Sir George Thomas Staunton

Sir George Thomas Staunton (1781–1859), Sinologist and politician, was a key figure in early nineteenth-century Anglo-Chinese relations. Staunton secured a post as a writer in the East India Company's factory in Canton in 1798 and was the only Englishman at the factory to study Chinese. He translated China's penal code and was promoted to chief of the Canton factory in 1816. He was a member of Britain's Amherst embassy to Peking in 1816–17 to protest against mandarins' treatment of Canton merchants. The embassy failed to obtain an imperial interview but, despite being threatened with detention by the Chinese, Staunton insisted that the British should not submit to the emperor. Staunton returned to England in 1817, and served as a Tory MP between 1818 and 1852. Staunton's *Memoirs*, which were printed privately in 1856, provide a unique insight into nineteenth-century British perceptions of China.

Cambridge University Press has long been a pioneer in the reissuing of out-of-print titles from its own backlist, producing digital reprints of books that are still sought after by scholars and students but could not be reprinted economically using traditional technology. The Cambridge Library Collection extends this activity to a wider range of books which are still of importance to researchers and professionals, either for the source material they contain, or as landmarks in the history of their academic discipline.

Drawing from the world-renowned collections in the Cambridge University Library, and guided by the advice of experts in each subject area, Cambridge University Press is using state-of-the-art scanning machines in its own Printing House to capture the content of each book selected for inclusion. The files are processed to give a consistently clear, crisp image, and the books finished to the high quality standard for which the Press is recognised around the world. The latest print-on-demand technology ensures that the books will remain available indefinitely, and that orders for single or multiple copies can quickly be supplied.

The Cambridge Library Collection will bring back to life books of enduring scholarly value (including out-of-copyright works originally issued by other publishers) across a wide range of disciplines in the humanities and social sciences and in science and technology.

Memoirs of the Chief Incidents of the Public Life of Sir George Thomas Staunton

One of the King's Commissioners to the Court of Pekin, and Afterwards for Some Time Member of Parliament for South Hampshire

George Thomas Staunton

CAMBRIDGE
UNIVERSITY PRESS

CAMBRIDGE UNIVERSITY PRESS

Cambridge, New York, Melbourne, Madrid, Cape Town, Singapore,
São Paolo, Delhi, Dubai, Tokyo

Published in the United States of America by Cambridge University Press, New York

www.cambridge.org
Information on this title: www.cambridge.org/9781108014922

© in this compilation Cambridge University Press 2010

This edition first published 1856
This digitally printed version 2010

ISBN 978-1-108-01492-2 Paperback

SIR GEORGE THOMAS STAUNTON, BAR.ᵗ

Anno Ætatis, 52.

MEMBER OF PARLIAMENT FOR SOUTH HAMPSHIRE.

From a small Portrait by Sir George Hayter

Memoirs

OF

THE CHIEF INCIDENTS OF THE PUBLIC LIFE

OF

SIR GEORGE THOMAS STAUNTON, BART.

HON. D.C.L. OF OXFORD;

ONE OF THE KING'S COMMISSIONERS TO THE COURT OF PEKIN,
AND AFTERWARDS FOR SOME TIME MEMBER OF
PARLIAMENT FOR SOUTH HAMPSHIRE,
AND FOR THE BOROUGH OF
PORTSMOUTH.

———

Printed for Private Circulation.

———

LONDON:

L. BOOTH, 307 REGENT STREET.

1856.

CONTENTS.

ERRATA.

Page 117, line 8, *for* eighteen *read* twenty-four.
  ,, 182, ,, 21, *for* solicit *read* admit.

NOTES, &c.

ON the 10th of November, 1836, in the fifty-sixth year of my age, at a period of little exciting occupation, and, therefore, so far favourable to a calm retrospect of past events, I commenced a register of a few of the chief incidents of my life, which has been continued from time to time down to my final retirement from public life, in July 1852.

I hope it may not prove altogether uninteresting to trace the steps by which I have successively attained my present position in society: first, in China, by giving to the European world the original translation of the Ta Tsing-leu-lee, or Penal Code of China, and afterwards obtaining the chief direction of our Chinese commerce, with the appointment of second Royal Commissioner to the

Court of Pekin, and eventually to the chief post in the Embassy, in the event of the death or coming away of the Ambassador. In the second place, in England, I gained the representation of South Hampshire, after a severe contest; and subsequently occupied that of the important naval station of Portsmouth, which I held unanimously, during three successive Parliaments, and in which I trust I have not been unworthily employed.

I was born on the 26th of May, 1781, at Milford, near Salisbury, in the house of my maternal grandfather, Benjamin Collins, Esq., a banker of considerable wealth and eminence in that city. My father had embarked for India with Lord Macartney in the preceding month of January, and it was proposed that my mother should follow him to that country as soon as possible after her confinement. In contemplation of this event I was sent over to Galway in Ireland, in the charge of a nurse, when only a few months old, and confided to the care of my paternal grandmother, Mrs. Staunton. Circumstances subsequently oc-

curred to prevent my mother from going out
to India, and my father returned from that
country in January 1785 : but I remained in
Ireland, in the charge of my grandmother,
until her decease in September 1784. I was
then sent back to England, and my father, on
his arrival from India, found me with my
mother at Milford; and saw me (now between
three and four years old) for the first time.
I must here affectionately record, that from
this moment, down to the latest period of
his life, the master purpose of my father's
mind was my education and welfare. A
difference of opinion may, perhaps, exist
respecting the wisdom and expediency of
deviating as much as he did from the cus-
tomary routine of education; but with regard to the excellence of the *ends* he had in
view there can be no question, and I should
be the most ungrateful of sons if I did not
here acknowledge my happiness in having
had, in him and in my dear mother, the best
and most affectionate of parents.

My father's earliest feelings on the subject

of my education are happily expressed in the following extract from his note-book, dated May 27th, 1788 :—

"Hier mon fils est entré dans sa huitième année. Je compte à l'avenir écrire un Journal, qui le regardera entièrement. Il naquît lorsque j'étois dans l'Inde. Il avoit plus de trois ans et demi avant que je l'ai vû. Depuis ce tems-là, j'ai tâché d'user des moyens d'éducation, [qui tendîssent à le rendre dans la suite, sage, sain, et savant. Sagesse comprend vertu ; vertu, absence des vices.

"Un de mes premiers soins étoit de lui inspirer une horreur et un mépris contre le mensonge, un des premiers vices des enfans, et qui est très naturel aux faibles de tous les âges, étant le moyen le plus simple d'éviter la punition des faits défendus par les forts. Il m'a été d'autant moins difficile de l'engager à être toujours véridique, qu'il n'étoit guères dans le cas de craindre, même des reproches pour les petits maux qui cause souvent l'étourderie des enfans, et dont je ne prenois jamais notice.

"Au reste, je compris bientôt combien il étoit essentiel de ne point lui donner, ni lui laisser donner, des mauvaises exemples : et j'ai taché de mettre plus de précaution dans toute ma conduite. La conversation qui n'est point adressée aux enfans, fait plus d'impression sur eux, que les préceptes qui leur sont adressés; et qu'ils soupçonnent toujours. Je pris donc soin que les sentimens que j'exprimois en sa présence étoit ceux que je voulois lui inspirer, et je recommandois les mêmes soins à sa mère, et aux autres avec lesquels il se trouvoit quelquefois."

It was no part of my father's plan to send me to a public school. Soon after the date of the above memorandum a private tutor was engaged, who lived in the house, and gave me instructions in the Classics; and I received lessons in other branches of knowledge from masters who visited me at stated hours for that purpose. From the age of ten to sixteen my tutor was John Christian Huttner, Esq., a German scholar, from the University of Leipsic, who is still living in this country, and has held with credit for many years the post of Translator at the Foreign Office.

One of my father's favourite objects was to familiarise my mind at a very early period with the rudiments of those sciences in which

instruction (if imparted at all) is usually
reserved for riper years. I was accordingly
taken, while a mere child, to the lectures of
Dr. Sibthorpe on Botany, Dr. Higgins on
Chemistry, and Dr. Thompson on Minera-
logy; and also occasionally to the meetings of
the Royal Society. My father also made, in
the year 1791, the tour of England and a
part of Scotland, for the express purpose of
showing to me the arts, manufactures, and
natural curiosities, of the different parts of
the country through which we travelled.
My mind, he hoped, would be thus stored
with new ideas, at the same time that my
bodily health would be strengthened by exercise. My father was strongly impressed
with the opinion that the innate curiosity
of children ought not to be thrown away
or corrupted with fairy tales and other ex-
travagances of the imagination; and that it
might be directed as agreeably, as well as
much more profitably, to the contemplation
of the wonderful realities of nature.

Another peculiarity in my father's system

of education was the treating the Latin and Greek in all respects as *living* languages, and the preponderance he gave to the prose classics over the poetical. Although much may be said in favour of this system in the abstract, it is not altogether suited to the established standard of classical taste in this country. The utmost familiarity with the best Latin and Greek prose writers will never be accepted as any compensation for an imperfect or superficial knowledge of the ancient poets.

I find in the memoirs of the late Sir James Smith, lately published, a letter from the late John Symmons, Esq., of Paddington House, containing the following amusing notice of me and my education about this period.

" *London, September 30th*, 1794.

"I have seen Sir George Staunton, but not so much of him as I could have wished; enough, however, to know that he has not visited the capital of China without making such observations as cannot but prove highly interesting in the detail, and from which I flatter myself with the hope of much delight and information at some future time, when both of us are less occupied than at present. His little boy comes with his tutor to my garden every day, and goes over the collection of plants in a regular course, with a Linnæus and a Hortus Kewensis in his hand. His memory is great, and his apprehension quick and lively, so that there can be little doubt of his progress in that, or any other study to which he applies his mind. But I have fears for his health, which seems but ill established, and cannot, in my judgment, be bene-fited by those continued attentions to all that diversity of languages and sciences which the Baronet is perpetually pouring into him. The vessel is certainly of fine but of delicate materials, and may be prematurely broken by too frequent use."—Vol. i. p. 304.

It is probable that the *friend* who accom-panied me to Mr. Symmons's garden, and who is improperly described as "tutor," was Mr. (now Sir John) Barrow, a gentleman whose valuable instructions in early youth, and many testimonies of cordial and constant friendship in after-life, I gratefully acknow-ledge. His singular genius and abilities were

at this early period fully appreciated by my
father, and, by his suggestion, he was appointed to accompany Lord Macartney's
Chinese Embassy, in which he rendered
those valuable services which led to his
subsequent official employment at the Cape
of Good Hope, and ultimately to his long
and distinguished official career at home, as
second Secretary of the Admiralty.

About two years before the letter just
quoted was written, an event occurred,
(namely, the appointment of my father as
Secretary of Legation, and eventual successor
of Lord Macartney as Ambassador to the
Court of Pekin,) which not only materially
influenced all the subsequent events of my
life, but proved the primary source of whatever reputation in the world, literary or
political, it has been my fortune to acquire.
Even with respect to my father, although his
character and reputation as a public man
were long before well established, he will
probably be better known to posterity as

the historian of the First British Embassy
to China, than as the negotiator of the treaty
with Tippoo Sultan, although that treaty
gave peace to India, and earned for him a
Baronetcy.

The first stipulation which my father
made, when the appointment to China was
offered to him, was, that I, together with
my tutor, Mr. Huttner, should be permitted
to accompany the expedition. My father
also took me with him upon his previous
journey to Naples in the spring of 1792,
for the purpose of procuring Chinese interpreters from the College of the Propaganda.
The impression which this journey, through
some of the most interesting parts of France,
Italy, and Germany, made upon my mind,
young as I was, was very vivid, and is even
yet by no means altogether obliterated. I
still remember to have seen the unhappy
royal family of France at the chapel of the
Tuileries; and to have been present at the
turbulent debates of the First National
Assembly, and of the Jacobin Club. None

of my subsequent visits to the same countries, however agreeable or instructive they may have been, have left images on my mind of such deep interest. It was at Naples that I first saw any of the natives of China; and it was in the course of the journey home from thence to England, and the outward-bound voyage to China, which soon followed, that my ears were first familiarised to the sounds of a language in which, during the next five-and-twenty years of my life, I had so much exercise.

The expedition to China occupied about two years, having sailed from Portsmouth on the 26th of September, 1792, and arrived again at that port on its return to England, on the 6th of September, 1794.

In the authentic account of the proceedings of the Embassy, which was written by my father, and published in August 1797, he gratified his feelings by alluding to me, indirectly, in several passages, some of which I subjoin :—

"In the train of the Ambassador, also, was a

page, of years too tender not to have still occasion for a tutor, who was a foreign gentleman of parts and erudition; and it will be seen in the course of this work that neither he nor his pupil proved useless to the public."—Vol. i. p. 37.——

"—— The difficulty (that of procuring copies of Chinese papers) was however overcome by means of the youth formerly mentioned as page to the Ambassador, and who had acquired an uncommon facility in copying the Chinese character, beside having made progress enough in the language to serve sometimes as interpreter; and it was necessary to have recourse to him for copying out every subsequent paper that there was occasion to present in the Chinese language."—Vol. ii. p. 142.——

"—— His Imperial Majesty inquired whether any person of the Embassy understood the Chinese language; and being informed that the Ambassador's page, a boy then in his thirteenth year, had alone made some proficiency in it, the Emperor had the curiosity to have the youth brought up to the throne, and desired him to speak Chinese. Either what he said, or his modest countenance or manner, was so pleasing to his Imperial Majesty, that he took from his girdle a purse hanging from it, for holding areca nut, and presented it to him. Purses are the ribands of the Chinese monarch,

which he distributes as rewards of merit among
his subjects, but his own purse was deemed a
mark of personal favour, according to the ideas
of Eastern nations, among whom anything worn
by the person of the sovereign is prized beyond
all other gifts. It procured for the young favourite
the notice and caresses of many of the mandarins,
while others, perhaps, envied his good fortune.
The Imperial purse is not at all magnificent, being
of yellow silk, with blue embroidery, and some
Tartar characters worked into it."—Vol. ii. p. 235.

Æneas Anderson, the *unauthorised* historian
of the Embassy, relates the last-mentioned
anecdote as follows :—

" The Emperor, it was said, received the credentials of the Embassy with the most ceremonious
formality. All, however, that we could learn, as
a matter of indubitable certainty, was the notice
His Imperial Majesty was pleased to take of
Master Staunton, the son of Sir George Staunton.
He appeared to be very much struck with the
boy's vivacity and deportment, and expressed his
admiration of the faculty which the young gentleman possessed of speaking six different languages.
The Emperor, to manifest the approbation he felt
on the occasion, not only presented him with his

own hand a very beautiful fan, and several small embroidered bags and purses, but commanded the interpreter to signify that he thought very highly of his talents and appearance." — P. 148.

The above incident is also alluded to by my late distinguished friend, Mr. Marsden, in the following note to an introduction to his translation of the history of Marco Polo.

" It is impossible for those who have read the account of Lord Macartney's Embassy not to be struck with the resemblance between this scene (the introduction of Marco Polo at the Chinese court, when a youth, by his father,) and that which passed at Jehol, in 1793, when Sir George Staunton presented his son, the present Sir George Staunton, to the venerable Kien-long." — P. ix.

This occurrence is not specially noticed in the private journal of Lord Macartney, which was published in the appendix to the memoir of his life, by Sir John Barrow ; but his lordship alludes to my knowledge of the Chinese language in another place, in the following flattering terms : —

" Sir George Staunton's son, a boy of twelve
years old, during our passage from England,
learned in a few broken lessons from a very
cross master, and by his own attention, not only
such a *copia verborum* and phraseology as enabled
him to make himself understood, and to understand
others, when he arrived in China; but acquired
such a facility in writing the Chinese character,
that he copied all our diplomatic papers for the
Chinese government, (the Chinese writers being
afraid of their hands being known,) in so neat and
expeditious a manner as to occasion great astonishment among them; and here, in confirmation of
what I have said above, let me observe, that this
young gentleman possesses already five languages,
English, Latin, Greek, French, and Chinese, a
thing scarcely to be paralleled at so early an age."
—Vol. ii. p. 501.

Although I have undoubtedly derived
many advantages in after-life from the circumstance of my association in early youth
with this Chinese Embassy, it was at the
time, to my father, personally, the occasion
of much vexation and disappointment. In
consideration of his appointment to succeed
Lord Macartney as Resident Minister for

England at the court of Pekin, he had declined the far more lucrative post which had been offered to him of Chief of the Select Committee of the East India Company's supercargoes at Canton. Unfortunately, however, several unpropitious public events occurred at the period of the Embassy, which made it impossible for him to obtain permission to remain in an official capacity at Pekin after the departure of Lord Macartney; and, although the British government was afterwards disposed to have sent him again to China in the character of Minister Plenipotentiary, agreeably to an express invitation, which was received in 1796, from the Chinese court, he was unhappily disabled from again engaging in public life by a paralytic seizure, with which he was attacked very soon after his return to Europe. Under these circumstances it occurred to him that an appointment in the service of the East India Company might still enable me to follow up my early introduction to Chinese diplomacy, and to acquire honour and distinction in that career.

He accordingly applied to the Court of Directors for a writership to Canton, on the score of my knowledge of the Chinese language,—a qualification which, in the present day, is no very remarkable distinction; but in which, at that time, I stood absolutely alone, without a rival! The application was for a long time resisted as an undue interference with private patronage, and was only obtained through the most persevering exertions. I was appointed a writer to Canton on the 10th of April, 1798, and embarked for China in the Hindostan Indiaman, on the 18th of June, 1799.

My father, in thus parting with an only child under circumstances which left little hope of his ever seeing him again, made a most severe sacrifice of his personal feelings. But he saw no other road which promised so fair to enable me to maintain in after-life my rank and position in society. He saw that the moderate fortune he was enabled to leave me would render me too *wealthy* to be likely to pursue with success any laborious profes-

c

sion, and yet wholly inefficient adequately
to sustain my social position without one.
As, however, the question of a China appointment was for some time in suspense,
it was thought, in the meanwhile, advisable
that I should also qualify for the legal profession, by entering and keeping terms at
the Middle Temple ; but I never commenced
any regular course of legal study.

In September 1795, my father purchased
from Sir George Dallas, Bart. the house
No. 17 Devonshire Street, in which he and
my mother passed the remainder of their
lives, and in which, after the lapse of fifty
years, I still reside.

During the five years' interval between
my return with the Chinese Embassy to
Europe, and my re-embarkation for China,
in the service of the East India Company,
I remained constantly under the eyes of my
parents, except for a few months in the
summer of 1796 ; which I spent in the house
of the Rev. P. Brodie, at Winterslow, near
Salisbury.   This was almost the only op-

portunity which my father's system of education had hitherto allowed me of freely
associating with young persons of about my
own age: and I recollect, with peculiar
pleasure, the summer which I thus spent in
the society of the young Brodies, my cousins,
and in that of their guest and relative, Thomas Denman (now Lord Denman), Lord
Chief Justice of the Court of Queen's Bench.
The eldest of Mr. Brodie's sons is now at the
head of his profession as a conveyancer; the
second is a banker, and has long and honourably represented Salisbury, his native city, in
Parliament; and the third is the first surgeon
of the age, and a Baronet. The established
system, both of instruction and amusement,
under the Rev. Mr. Brodie's roof, was admirable. Kindness and discipline were happily blended, and the excellence of Mr.
Brodie's parental care and judgment has
happily received a practical confirmation in
the success in life of his children.

In February 1797, before I had completed

my sixteenth year, I was entered as a Fellow-
Commoner of Trinity College, Cambridge;
but whether my father had at that time any
intention of placing me permanently at the
University, I cannot say. His attention was
particularly drawn to Cambridge at that
moment by the high reputation of the lectures
which were given there on Arts and Manufactures by Professor Farish. The selection
of Trinity College was undoubtedly determined by the idea which he had entertained,
that I might claim some peculiar credit or
advantage in the College in the character
of Founder's kin, — one of my ancestors,
Harvey Staunton, having been the Founder
of Michael's Hall, which was afterwards
incorporated with Trinity College by Henry
the Eighth. The name of Harvey Staunton
is duly commemorated every day in the grace
said before meat in the College Hall, but his
kin was allowed no privileges. During the
few months that I continued at Cambridge, I
was occasionally the associate, though many
years younger in age, of the late Dr. Young,

the late Mr. Dodwell, the late Lord Congle-
ton, Sir Frederick Trench, Lords Brownlow,
Melbourne, and some others of that era; but
my comparative youth, and residence out of
the College with my parents, who had accompanied me to Cambridge, prevented my
forming with them any close intimacies or
connexions. It is not improbable, however,
that I might have pursued a University education at Cambridge for, at least, a couple
of years, if my father had not been disgusted
with what he considered as the injustice
done me in the distribution of prizes to
Freshmen on the first year's college ex-
amination. Nevertheless; as I was placed
on the *second*, out of the *five* classes into
which the young men of that year were
divided, I do not think that, considering
my having been so much younger than my
competitors, and having only kept *two* out
of three terms, I had much reason to complain. But my father (it having been admitted that I had made good my claim to
a prize in the *mathematical* department) was

indignant that I should have been excluded from the reward due to a first-class man, for the want of a few Latin verses; and he, therefore, at once withdrew my name from the books of the College.

————

At length the period arrived for my proceeding to my destination in China. My father and mother accompanied me to Portsmouth, and afterwards to Ryde in the Isle of Wight, and remained with me to the latest moment. My father's feelings on this occasion are best described in his own words, in the following extract from a letter which he penned the day after my departure:—

"*Upper Ryde, Isle of Wight, June* 19, 1799.

"I have to tell you, my dear George, though it will be long, very long, before you can know it, that your dear mother and I passed the remainder of yesterday, after your departure, very tolerably. After dinner we drove to St. Helen's, where we saw some of the ships, particularly the Hindostan, come to anchor; and we were not without hope of finding means of some communication with it, but

found soon afterwards that the fleet had sailed
away. All rejoice at the continuance of the fair
wind, and so ought I. Everything will, I hope,
turn out prosperously for you, and I still believe
that I have fallen upon the best, or at least the
most likely, means of providing for your future
happiness, but it is not the most happy for me to
be thus separated from you.

"I do not, my dear George, forgive myself for
not sufficiently impressing upon your mind, before
you left us, that your mother and I both most
heartily and sincerely wish that, the moment you
find yourself disgusted with your situation in
China, you will leave it and return to us. You
may rest perfectly assured that you will meet from
us a most hearty welcome, and that we shall not
only be reconciled to, but rejoice at any step you
take for your own satisfaction. We have, with
economy, a sufficient fortune for you; and something may, and certainly will, turn up at home, or
at least in Europe, that will add to your emolu-
ment and comfort. This letter will, I hope, not
reach you too late; you are sure of our perfect
approbation in anything you do.

"Young Mr. —— keeps a journal, as you do.
It is a practice highly useful, and ought to be
continued; there is, however, no general rule
without an exception, much fatigue or occupation

may justly prevent it. There is nothing that I recommend to you but you may have sufficient reason for not doing, and, if not done, I shall always suppose you right, and be satisfied. One person cannot do all that might be supposed good to do, and must therefore decline some part. It will be good to improve in the Chinese, both with a view to the time you may remain in the country, and to the advantage and credit of it afterwards ; but I do not pretend to lay down rules for what is to be done by you : your own good sense and prudence will direct you for the best. All I beg is that you will not exert yourself too much, for fear of affecting your health. Mr. Henry Browne has lately purchased the seat of North Mims in Hertfordshire. You, my dear George, will not stay in China to acquire as much as he has done, but you will finally return, I hope, with a competent fortune, and the acquisition of so much knowledge as will give you an *éclat* peculiar to yourself. The addition of my fortune will come to you, dignified by your own character, as well as Title and good family. May my wishes for you be gratified to the utmost extent, and may you be substantially happy and good ! This is the anxious and constant prayer of your most affectionate father,

(Signed) GEORGE LEONARD STAUNTON."

The advantages which my father affectionately anticipated may fairly be said to have
been in the end fully realized. At the ex-
piration of eighteen years, I finally returned to
England from China with a handsome addition
to my patrimonial fortune; and (I trust I
may add) with the credit of duties faithfully
discharged and an unimpeached character.
But the apprehensions which he also entertained, that I might, in the first instance, feel
disgusted with my new position, were but too
well founded. The period of the two first
years which I spent in China was certainly
the most gloomy period of my life. My abrupt removal from the roof of affectionate and
indulgent parents to a very remote establishment, and a society of a very peculiar kind,
and of total strangers, was of itself sufficiently
painful. In addition to this, my private and
perhaps over-refined system of education had
rendered me singularly unprepared for those
collisions which always must attend a youth's
first initiation in mixed society. Unfortunately also for me, no favourable preposses-

sions smoothed my way and ushered me into
the microcosm of the British Factory, in which
I was now to be incorporated. The *principle*
itself of my appointment was unpopular. A
writership to China, being the most valuable
portion of East Indian patronage, had been
generally reserved for the sons and relatives
of the Directors; and the exception which had
been made in my favour, on the special ground
of my knowledge of the Chinese language,
could not but be felt to be a tacit reproach to
those, who, with greater opportunities than I
had, had omitted to render themselves equally
qualified. There was, lastly, at that period,
a certain coarseness and freedom of manners
prevailing in the establishment, which happily
disappeared a few years after, but which was
peculiarly shocking to my inexperience, on
my first introduction. Nevertheless, I formed
some early friendships in China, which still
subsist; and although I am fully conscious
that I was not at first generally popular, I
have had the gratification of receiving, on the
occasion of my *final* retirement from the

service, a more signal testimonial of regard
and esteem from the circle in which I had
dwelt, than had ever been conferred, even
on the most popular of my predecessors.

Amongst the early occasions of disgust
which I felt, was the nature of my employment. The junior members of the establishment were chiefly engaged in the *necessary*,
but not very agreeable or intellectual,
functions of superintending the weighing
of goods, and in the transcription of commercial documents. I was, however, often
called to higher things. A few days after
my arrival in China, in January 1800,
serious disputes happened to arise between
the British authorities and the Chinese provincial government. The advantage of pos-
sessing, under such circumstances, a confidential interpreter within our own English
circle, instead of exclusively confiding, as
heretofore, in native linguists, who might
be corrupted or intimidated, was at once
fully appreciated. The following official
report of my first services in China was

addressed by the Select Committee at Canton
to the Court of Directors in England, on the
26th of May, 1800 :—

" We cannot dismiss this subject without con-
veying our testimony and satisfaction at the attention Mr. Staunton pays to his improvement in the
language of the country, nor contemplate but with
pleasure the use he has, and may hereafter be of
in any negotiations with the Chinese government ;
in proof of which we need only observe that, at the
last conference, on the 9th of April, the Mandarine
was not desirous that any Hong merchant should
attend. We understand likewise that he has some
prospect of obtaining a copy of the famous Chinese
code, so highly extolled in the French work,
' Mémoires sur les Chinois,' in which case, perhaps,
the honour is reserved for him of supplying in
time several desiderata in literature."

My father lived to have the satisfaction
of hearing of my safe arrival in China, and
was much gratified by the reports which
reached him from various quarters of the
evidence I had so soon an opportunity of
giving of my proficiency in the Chinese language, and of the flattering notice that had

been taken of it. He, however, gradually sunk under his increasing infirmities, and died at his house in Devonshire Street, on the 14th of January, 1801. I was named in his will one of his executors, and also residuary legatee; and the other executors having thought it best, under these circumstances, to decline acting, they left me singly to prove the Will. To enable me to do so, permission was applied for and immediately obtained from the Court of Directors of the East India Company for my return to England. I accordingly left China, after about two years' residence, in January 1802, in company with the late Richard Hall, Esq., many years Chief of the Factory, a gentleman to whose personal kindness and encouragement upon my first joining the establishment I must ever acknowledge myself much indebted. His successor, James Drummond, Esq. (now Viscount Strathallan) was, in the sequel, no less friendly to me; and, in one of his earliest despatches to the Court of Directors, he expressed his regret at my absence in the following terms :—

" The absence of Sir George Staunton at this moment cannot be sufficiently lamented, as we had every right to expect the most essential advantages would have been derived from his knowledge and abilities."—*Canton, April* 16th, 1802.

I arrived in England in June 1802, a few days after I had become of age, and I was indulged with the permission to remain at home two years. I lived during that period chiefly in the society of my mother, my other near relatives, and my father's numerous personal friends; all of whom greeted my return amongst them with great cordiality and kindness. The most distinguished amongst my late father's personal friends at that period was the late Earl of Macartney, who obtained from the East India Company my permission to return to Europe, and announced it to me in a very kind letter, of which the following is the concluding paragraph :—

" Wishing you a pleasant voyage, and a happy return to your country and friends, and assuring you of my earnest desire to supply to you, as far as in my power, the place of your excellent father, I remain, with the truest esteem and regard,

" My dear Sir George, your most sincere Friend,

(Signed)   " MACARTNEY."

In the month of December 1802, Lord Macartney presented me to their late Majesties George III. and Queen Charlotte at St. James's ; and I was soon after indebted to his Lordship for (what has always been considered a very flattering literary distinction) my election into the club founded by Dr. Johnson, commonly called the Literary Club. I was also about this time elected a Fellow of the Royal Society, through the friendly exertions of my late excellent friend, Dr. Maton.

In the autumn of this year, as soon as the routine of business connected with the proving of my father's will was over, I went over to Ireland for the purpose of taking possession of my patrimonial property of Cargin, in the county

of Galway, and of becoming personally acquainted with my Irish friends and relatives,
and with my tenantry.   In the course of the
ensuing London winter I had the gratification,
on arriving at man's estate, of associating
with all those friends who had only known
me three years before as a *boy :* and, as far
as I recollect, the "young Baronet" was
generally well received.

At length, however, in June 1804, my
leave of absence expired, and it became
necessary that I should return without further
delay to my station in the service of the East
India Company in China, — a station of
which I had, in fact, as yet only experienced
the labour and inconveniences, without reap-
ing the profits.   I was, however, in this
year, advanced from the rank of *writer* to
that of *supercargo*.   This latter title is not
very dignified, nor at all correctly descriptive
of the nature of the duties to be performed;
but it was to me of essential importance, as
it guaranteed to me a salary increasing according to seniority from *two* to *ten* thousand

a-year. I arrived in China in December, 1804, and remained till January 1808, when I availed myself of a privilege which was enjoyed by all the supercargoes in succession, of visiting Europe once in the course of their term of residence without any forfeiture of pay.

During these three years spent in China, besides my occasional duties of Chinese translation and interpretation, whenever discussions took place with the officers of the Chinese government, I filled the situation of secretary to the Select Committee; an office which gave me constant and ample occupation, and made me officially cognisant of all the most important and confidential transactions of the establishment. I had also the gratification, in 1805, of contributing to the introduction into China of the method of Vaccine Inoculation, by means of a short treatise on the subject, composed by Mr. Pearson, the surgeon of the Factory, which, by the assistance of a native, I was enabled to translate into Chinese, and to print for general circulation.

D

34 MEMOIRS.

The communications of the British Factory with the Chinese provincial government, though frequent, were not of much importance, until February, 1807, when, an affray having occurred between a party of British sailors and the Chinese populace, in the course of which a native was killed, the British trade was suspended for about six weeks, and a peremptory demand made for the discovery and surrender of the culprit by the Chinese authorities, which at one time threatened very serious consequences. The affair was ultimately compromised by the Chinese authorities fixing on an individual at random, and at the same time pronouncing his acquittal on the plea of accident.

In respect to the part I took in bringing about this arrangement the Select Committee were pleased to report to the Court of Directors as follows:—

"No expression can too strongly mark the importance of the assistance received on this trying occasion from Sir George Staunton."

This commendation was fully responded

to by the East India Directors in the following terms, in their dispatch of the 26th of
February, 1808 : —

   " We cannot too strongly notice the value of
the assistance you received from Sir George Staunton, whose knowledge of the Chinese language
enabled him to give a faithful interpretation of
your sentiments to the Mandarines, which, but for
him, we have every reason to believe would not
have been done, as neither the linguists nor the
merchants can venture to do it, when those sentiments are displeasing to the Mandarines, and we
are concerned to say that none of our other servants are qualified to do it.
   " We have appointed Sir George Staunton
Chinese Interpreter to the Factory, with a salary
of five hundred pounds per annum, to be paid out
of the Commission, as a mark of our approbation
of his conduct, and a stimulus to some of our
junior servants to qualify themselves to succeed
him hereafter."

   This appointment was not of much importance to me in a pecuniary point of view, as
I relinquished its emoluments, after the first
year, in favour of the Rev. Dr. Morrison;
but the testimony it conveyed in so marked

a manner of the approbation of the Court of Directors was very gratifying.

It was in the spring of this year (1807) that I became first acquainted with the Rev. Dr. Morrison, through the medium of a letter from Sir Joseph Banks, which he presented to me upon his first arrival in China as a missionary. From that period down to that of his lamented decease, in 1834, I was in constant communication with him, either personally or by letter. I was invariably his *friend* and *advocate*, and, considering the official position I held in China, I might add *patron*. I was the first to present him to the Chief of the Factory, Mr. Roberts; who, upon my special recommendation, conferred upon him an office in the service of the East India Company, which he continued to hold as long as they had any establishment in China; and, in fact, until within a few days of his death. Dr. Morrison always acknowledged his obligations to me in the most grateful manner, and I should not have thought it necessary to dwell so much on the subject if some of his injudicious friends and historians had not appeared to wish to keep his connexion with me out of sight, and to entertain the absurd idea that there could possibly have ever existed a *rivalry* between us. I was certainly several years prior to him in the field, but I cultivated the Chinese language altogether for different purposes, and much less exclusively and assiduously than he did, and I therefore freely, and with pleasure, acknowledge that he attained ultimately to a much greater degree of proficiency.

During my absence from England at this period, I lost my father's early and distinguished friend, the Earl of Macartney, who died at his house in Curzon Street, in March 1806. Their acquaintance commenced at Granada, upon Lord Macartney's appointment to the government of that island in 1774, where my father had been previously established some years, and had held high office. This acquaintance soon ripened into an intimacy, which ceased only with their lives. My father was certainly indebted to Lord Macartney for his subsequent appointments to India and China, but the benefits conferred by this association were *mutual*. Lord Macartney could not have gone out to India at all if my father had not, with great exertion and address, successfully negotiated his Lordship's exchange at the Court of the Tuileries, for he was, at the period of his nomination to the government of Madras, still a prisoner of war, though allowed to visit in London on his parole.

There is also good evidence to show, that if it had not been for my father's exertions and talents his Lordship might very probably have experienced the fate of his unfortunate predecessor Lord Pigot, and have been sent to England a degraded prisoner, by General Stuart, instead of returning, as he did, in due time, with a spotless fame, and the credit of a successful administration. And even with respect to the subsequent Chinese Embassy, I am satisfied that the credit obtained by his Lordship on the occasion is very considerably owing to the advice he received from my father during the mission, and the impression produced by the very able narrative of it he afterwards published. Lord Macartney had no share whatever in obtaining for my father the Baronetcy and the pension, which were conferred on him for his successful treaty with Tippoo; and although Lord Macartney certainly did apply both to Mr. Fox and Mr. Pitt for some further employment for my father, worthy of his high character and former services, those applications were not successful. I do not make these remarks in order to depreciate Lord Macartney's friendship and good wishes, but only to show that the term *patron*, which some persons have presumptuously applied to him in relation to my father, is wholly inapplicable.

My situation in China, from 1804 to 1808, though far less irksome than upon my former visit, was always felt by me as a painful sacrifice; and the period of the summer recess at Macao, which to others was a source of enjoyment, was to me, owing to the oppressive heat of a tropical climate, and the listlessness attending the suspension of ordinary employments, more distasteful than even the labours and confinement of Canton. In 1806 I was tempted for a few months to join some of my associates in rather high play, but I have great pleasure in recording that I had very soon the fortitude to break off from this pernicious practice at once, and for ever.

About this time I carried on an interesting correspondence with the late Sir James Mackintosh, then a Judge at Bombay. The correspondence commenced with a request on his part that I would execute certain commissions for him in China, and he reminded me in his letter of the precept of Scripture, " Thy friend and thy father's friend forget not." In 1807 I entertained for some weeks at my house at Macao a namesake of his, whom he had recommended to my civilities.

I arrived in England in June 1808, and remained till April 1810. During this interval my social position with my mother, relatives, and friends, was much the same as it had been when at home some years before; but I was also engaged in some literary and diplomatic projects connected with China, which it is necessary to notice.

It was naturally a very favourite project with me to endeavour to urge upon the consideration of the Government and the East India Company the expediency of renewing our diplomatic relations with the Court of Pekin, with the view of improving our commercial position at Canton. The favourable notice of my services in the provincial negotiations at Canton encouraged me to hope that I might be able to render important services to my country, if more extended opportunities were opened to me through the medium of a public mission to Pekin. My endeavours to bring this subject before the official authorities in England were warmly seconded by my excellent friend,

Mr. (now Sir John) Barrow; and, in 1809, the necessity of taking some step of this nature was strengthened by an apprehension which then existed, that the Court of Pekin might resent our occupation for some months of the Portuguese settlement of Macao, in defiance of the Canton authorities, unless some suitable explanation were given. The Chairman of the Court of Directors accordingly sent for me,' and, after acquainting me that it was in contemplation to send a mission to Pekin, consisting of two commissioners, of which I was to be one, requested me to furnish him with a detailed plan of operations, for his information and that of the Government. This I did accordingly, and very soon after I received a letter from my friend, Mr. Barrow, of which the following is an extract:—

" (*Most Secret.*)   *Admiralty*, 10*th Nov.* 1809.

   " My dear Sir George,

      " We have done the deed; and I most heartily congratulate you on the almost certain prospect of your going to Pekin as the King's

ambassador. Since I received the enclosed, Mr.
Dundas has been with me here, and informed
me that, in consequence of my communication
to Lord Harrowby, his Lordship and he thought
proper to send for the chairs; that they all entirely
concurred with me in the necessity of doing something, and doing it speedily, to prevent the ill
consequences that might be expected from a
measure (the Macao expedition) which His Majesty's Government had, in fact, been at great
pains to prevent; that they also concurred with
me that *the only person to be thought of for a*
mission to Pekin was Sir George Staunton, and
that he would be sent for immediately. He told
me, moreover, that preparations would immediately
be set on foot, and asked me if I did not think
you might go out in the man-of-war, which would
convoy out the spring fleet. I told him that I
conceived this would, on many accounts, be the
best opportunity."

A short time after receiving this letter
I was sent for by the Chairman of the Court
of Directors; but, instead of receiving the
expected invitation, was coolly informed that,
although my plan of a mission had been ap-
proved, I could not be employed upon it,
as, upon further consideration, it was thought

most advisable not to include in it any person who was actually in the service of the East India Company.

It is impossible to express the mortification and irritation of mind which I felt at this most unlooked-for communication; and I must say that now, coolly reflecting upon it, after a lapse of six-and-thirty years, I still think I was extremely ill used, and the victim of some unworthy intrigue, which it is now of little consequence to attempt to unravel. As, however, the plan of a mission to Pekin was soon after abandoned altogether, (until my ultimate appointment in 1816) my feelings on my intended exclusion from it, were, of course, a good deal mitigated.

At this period I had another object of pursuit, which occupied a good deal more of my time, and which, although not so exciting at the moment, may, perhaps, confer more repute on my name than any other incident of my life: I mean the publication of my translation of the *Ta Tsing leu-lee*, or Penal Code of China. I commenced this work during the summer at Macao, and completed it on board ship in the course of the homeward voyage. The copyright was sold to Cadell and Davies, the booksellers, for five hundred pounds; and it was printed by them in rather too expensive a style, in order to correspond in size with the quarto volumes of my father's account of Lord Macartney's Embassy. The preparation of the preface, and the appendix of miscellaneous documents, occupied a considerable time, so that the volume was not finally before the public till March 1810. It was not to be expected that a work of this nature would be generally popular, or often found upon drawing-room tables; but in the literary world it was received with a degree of favour and indulgence which exceeded my most sanguine expectations. The manner in which it has since been occasionally quoted and referred to, encourages me, at the end of five-and-thirty years, to flatter myself that it now possesses a fixed and respectable position in our Oriental literature.

It has also latterly acquired a practical value as a *Law Book*, which I certainly could not have anticipated. Sir Ralph Rice informs me that he had perpetually occasion to refer to my translation of the Chinese Penal Code when administering the law to the Chinese community in the capacity of Chief Justice of Prince of Wales Island. Still more recently Sir John Davis informs me that my work is constantly in the hands of the Chief Justice of Hong Kong for a similar purpose.

I cannot refuse myself the gratification of here recording the flattering testimonies of some of the principal Reviews, omitting only that of the " Quarterly," which, having been written by Mr. Barrow, may be supposed to have been influenced by the partiality of private friendship.

Edinburgh Review.

" It is rather remarkable that, notwithstanding the great commercial intercourse which England has now maintained with China for more than a century, the work before us should have been the very first ever rendered out of that language directly into our own. It appears to us, however, to be at least as important in itself as it is remarkable for its rarity. It contains, as the title imports, the authentic text of the whole Penal Law of China; and, as their peculiar system of jurisprudence has attached a certain public punishment to the violation or neglect of almost every civil obligation, their Penal Law comprises an incidental view of their whole system of legislation. Now there is certainly no one document from which we may form a judgment of the character and condition of a nation with so much safety as from the body of their laws; and when these are presented to us, not in the partial abstracts of their admirers or detractors, but in the original fulness and nakedness of their authentic statutes, the information which they afford may be fairly considered as paramount to all that may be derived from other sources. The representations of travellers, even where their fidelity is liable to no impeachment, will almost always take a tinge from their own imagination or affections; and where enthusiasm or controversy have any place in the discussion, there is an end to all prospect of accuracy or justice. The laws of a people, however, are actual specimens of their intellect and character, and may lead the reflecting observer, to whom they are presented, in any corner of the

world, to a variety of important conclusions that
did not occur to the individual by whom they
were collected.   In such a work the legislator
inevitably paints both himself and the people for
whom he legislates ; and, as nothing here depends
upon the colouring of style or ornament, nothing
short of intentional fabrication in the translator
can prevent us from forming a correct notion of
the original.   In the case before us, however, we
have not only every reason to believe that the
translation is perfectly just and accurate, but
think we can discover in the translator such
candour and coolness of judgment as would entitle
him to be trusted in a matter of far greater temp-
tation.   Sir George Staunton, in an introduction
of considerable length, but which, its clearness,
modesty, and intelligence, made us wish longer,
has presented us with an interesting sketch of the
general character of the Chinese Institutions, and
endeavoured, though with a visible leaning in their
favour, to mediate between those who had exag-
gerated their pretensions, and those who had been
offended at the disappointment of extravagant expectations."   *August* 1810.   Page 478.

Eclectic Review.

" If our Baronets in general were to employ
their time as well as Sir George Staunton, and

consider it fashionable to be a Fellow of the Royal
Society, rather than a member of White's Club,
or a subscriber at Brookes's, we suspect philoso-
phers would learn to think more reverently of
hereditary distinctions. The work before us is
the result of extraordinary attainments, so dili-
gently and judiciously employed as to render an
important service to the literary public. Scarcely
any other individual was, perhaps, equally competent to the task, nor would any one have done
wisely to undertake it who could not afford to
spend his time in the acquisition of an unprofitable
celebrity. It is not within reach of the more
numerous classes of the community ; and, indeed,
the entertainment it affords is too scanty, and
the instruction, small as it is, too recondite, to
attract attention from general readers. It is a
valuable addition, however, to English literature ;
it is a curiosity which will enrich the museum of
our moral history, and assist philosophic investi-
gations, though not adapted for general use. The
purposes it may answer are not of essential importance, but they are such as could not be
answered by any other means."—1810, p. 143.

Monthly Review.

" We hail the work before us, the first-fruits
of his (Sir George Staunton's) more intimate ac-

quaintance with the inhabitants of China, as reflecting honour on the liberality of the Company,
on the good sense exhibited by the translator
himself in the choice of a subject; and, above
all, on the provident sagacity of the Parent by
whom he was qualified and prepared to strike
out this honourable course of useful celebrity,
and whose worth and talents were personally
known to us."—P. 114.

Critical Review.

" Our sense of obligation to the translator of
the Chinese Code (who inherits the spirit of en-
quiry and intelligence, together with the Title, of
his late respected father), is not at all lessened
by the opinion we entertain of the Chinese character."—P. 340.

British Critic.

" We heartily wish success to Sir George
Staunton in the literary career he has marked
out for himself, and consider him as entitled to
the best thanks of the public, for putting it in
possession of a mass of valuable information, from
which it had hitherto been totally excluded. The
documents contained in the appendix, translated
from Chinese originals, will not be found the
least interesting part of the work, which they
tend materially to elucidate." —P. 224.

Lastly, the following extract from the Review of the celebrated Chinese and Oriental scholar, Mr. Klaproth, establishes the perfect fidelity of the English version :—

"Je n'ai qu'à citer Sir George Thomas Staunton, et Mr. Manning. Je reçus à Saint-Pétersbourg, en 1810, la version du Code Pénal de la Chine faite par Sir George. Je l'ai soigneusement comparée avec l'original, et j'ai été frappé de son exactitude ; aussi n'ai-je pas manqué de rendre publiquement à l'auteur de ce travail important, les éloges qu'il mérite à si juste titre."

Journal Asiatique, 1829, p. 6.

In the autumn of 1809 I made a tour through some of the central counties of England, and visited, amongst other places, Staunton Hall, near Newark, in Nottinghamshire, the ancient residence and property of the eldest branch of my family. It is a handsome Gothic mansion, built, or rather re-built, in 1558; and the estate, which is considerable, has been held by the Stauntons in direct lineal descent from one generation to another for no less than six hundred and

twenty-two years; when, by the death of
Harvey Staunton, Esq., without male issue,
in 1688, the eldest branch became extinct in
the male line. It then descended by females
to the Charltons, and, in 1807, passed by the
will of the heiress of the Charltons to her
cousin Elisabeth, the wife of the Rev. Dr.
Aspinshawe, who was directed to take the
name and bear the arms of Staunton. On
the death of Thomas Staunton, Esq., (member for Ipswich in England, and Galway
in Ireland,) in 1784, the second branch
of the Stauntons became also extinct in the
male line, and my father then became the
eldest, and indeed only male representative
of this very ancient family. An over-scru-
pulous delicacy had prevented my father
from ever making any advance towards an
acquaintance with the old lady, who left the
Staunton property to its present possessor;
but it was the opinion of a gentleman in
the neighbourhood, to whom I was introduced, and who had been well acquainted
with Mrs. Charlton, that her regard and vene-

ration for the original stock of the Staunton
family was such, that, if my father had made
himself personally known to her, she would
undoubtedly have left the property to him
in preference to any of her nearer female
relations. However this may be, and however flattering it might have been to my
personal vanity, as well as desirable as a
source of additional wealth, I very much
doubt whether my individual happiness and
comfort would have been promoted by an
establishment in *Nottinghamshire* rather than
in Hampshire, in which county I actually
purchased, in 1819, my present estate and
summer residence. I am quite sure that I
had a fortunate escape in 1818, when I was
overbid by Colonel Wildman in the offer I
made for Newstead Abbey. I was tempted
by its vicinity to the original seat of my ancestors, but it would have been injurious to me,
in a pecuniary point of view, even upon my
own terms; and an establishment so remote
from my present friends and connexions
would have been every way inconvenient.

I landed at Canton, upon my fourth voyage to China, in December 1810, and immediately resumed my former post of secretary to the Select Committee. It was the post in many respects best suited to me; and previous experience rendered its duties now comparatively easy. I had also the gratification of finding a gradual improvement in the tone and character of our English society in China, which tended to render my residence in that country less irksome. My distaste of my position in China, nevertheless, soon returned upon me with redoubled force; and, after a residence of only about fourteen months, I embarked for England, in January 1812, under a sick certificate. As my indisposition was not apparently severe, my renewed absence from my station thus early, gave rise to some animadversion. My defence is, that I only availed myself of a privilege which was equally open to every other member of the establishment, and made no claim to any special favour.

The only remarkable incident at this

period was the unusually familiar and friendly intercourse which, for a few months, subsisted between the British establishment and the Chinese authorities, and of which I happened to be, in some measure, the occasion. The circumstances are thus related in a letter from China, dated July 1811 : —

" The present Viceroy proves to be *Sung*, the mandarine who conducted the British Embassy, and was so highly spoken of by Lord Macartney. Hearing that Sir George Staunton was in the country, he immediately expressed a wish to see him. Sir George Staunton consequently went up from hence to Canton, and was received on the day of his arrival with distinguished marks of attention. He had three interviews, at one of which he dined with the Viceroy, by special invitation. The Viceroy having afterwards occasion to visit Macao, the Committee and Sir George called on him. To the surprise of everybody, the Viceroy very shortly called at the Factory to return the visit, when he partook of refreshments, and distributed little presents to all the party. From the character given of this remarkable personage, these distinguished marks of attention augur favourably, and it is thought that important advantages may result from his countenance and support."

There was certainly at this time, apparently, a most favourable opening for an improved system of intercourse between the English and the Chinese authorities; but, however good the Viceroy's intentions may have been, he had little opportunity for carrying them into effect, as he was recalled to Pekin in the course of the following winter, and matters immediately fell back into the old channel.

I landed in England, after a remarkably quick and pleasant voyage, on the 12th of May, 1812. My health and spirits were rapidly re-established by my return to my native air and by the cheering society of my relations and friends; and having by this time made a respectable addition to my fortune, I had certainly great temptations to relinquish any further connexion with China, where my position was still attended with so much sacrifice of personal comfort. On the other hand, my prospects in China had been improved by the retirement of several of my seniors on the establishment; and it was certainly desirable, not merely in a pecuniary view, but as conducive to my personal credit, that I should, previous to my final resignation of the service, hold, at least for a short time, the highest post in the British Factory. Under the influence of these considerations I embarked for China, for the fifth and last time, in April 1814.

The discussions which had previously taken place in 1813, relative to the renewal of the charter of the East India Company, naturally led to a call upon my services; and the East India Directors seemed to be well pleased to have had upon the spot at such a crisis, an individual whose local knowledge and experience seemed peculiarly to qualify him to explain and vindicate their policy and privileges in respect to Chinese commerce. An application was made to me officially by the President of the India Board, the Earl of Buckinghamshire, in the following terms :—

"*Nocton, Sept.* 2*d*, 1812.

"Sir,

"The weight I attach to the information in your power to afford upon the subject of China, I trust, will be deemed a sufficient apology for troubling you with this line, for the purpose of calling to your recollection an expectation you had allowed me to encourage, that you would have the goodness to commit to paper your ideas respecting the great question now pending of the China trade.

"Considerable pains have been taken, and are likely to be persevered in, in order to raise a clamour against the continuance of that trade exclusively in the hands of the East India Company ; and, as the arguments to be adduced upon the general principle against all monopolies are chiefly to be met by the special circumstances of the case arising out of the extraordinary system of the Chinese government, I am extremely desirous to have the benefit of your sentiments upon this important question, in any shape that may appear to you best calculated to assist me in the consideration of the subject, and as soon as may be consistent with your other avocations.

"I remain, &c. &c.,

(Signed) "BUCKINGHAMSHIRE.

"Sir George Staunton, Bart."

I accordingly drew up for his Lordship's information a memoir on the China trade, the receipt of which he acknowledged by the following note; and the memoir was soon after printed and circulated, for the information of the East India proprietors and of Parliament.

(*Private.*) "*India Board, Dec.* 2*d*, 1812.
" Sir,
"I have received and read your most excellent and able paper upon the subject of China, for which you will accept my most sincere acknowledgments. In the course of a few days I should wish to have some conversation with you upon it, and, with your permission, will appoint a time for that purpose.
"Most faithfully yours,
(Signed) "BUCKINGHAMSHIRE.
"Sir George Staunton, Bart."

I believe it is generally admitted that the memoir here adverted to, and the evidence which I afterwards gave to the committees on East Indian affairs of the two Houses of Parliament, had a considerable influence in

counteracting the clamour which was already
beginning to arise for throwing entirely open
the China trade; a measure which, on the
subsequent renewal of the charter, twenty
years after, new circumstances then rendered
unavoidable. I certainly do not contend
that all the arguments which I adduced in
1813 continued to be in equal force in 1833.
Time is unquestionably the greatest of inno-
vators. The system had so far broken down
that it no longer worked as well as it had
done; and the mere fact of the increased pre-
valence of public feeling against it was an
argument for its abandonment, but this great
change ought certainly to have been carried
into effect with more judgment and caution;
and the unhappy fate of the original Superin-
tendant of Trade, the unfortunate Lord Napier,
whose harassing disputes with the Government occasioned his illness, and, soon after,
his *death*, would then have been prevented.

Previous to my last embarkation for
China I paid a visit, in 1813, to my patrimonial property in Ireland, and made ar-

rangements with my tenants, which I hoped would in great measure prevent their suffering from the usual evils of absenteeism.

The period of my last residence in China, from September 1814 to January 1817, was by far the most active and anxious I passed in that country.

In consequence of the death or supercession of some of my seniors, I found myself, immediately on my arrival, associated in the Select Committee; and, in January 1816, I succeeded to the chiefship, in consequence of the retirement of Mr. Elphinstone. To this office was added, on the arrival of Lord Amherst, in the subsequent month of July, that of a King's Commissioner of Embassy. The duties of these appointments demanded all the energies of which my mind was capable. I found my colleagues in the Select Committee already involved in discussions with the Chinese provincial government of the most serious nature; and, a few days after I had landed at Macao, I was deputed by them to proceed to Canton, for the purpose of negotiating the adjustment of differences, and the vindication of proceedings, for which, although I had had no share in them, I was yet obliged in some degree to make myself responsible.

The position of the East India Company's servants in China at this time, is very fairly stated in the introductory chapter of Mr. Ellis's account of Lord Amherst's mission.

" The inflexible determination manifested by the Viceroy to persist in the acts complained of, compelled the supercargoes to have recourse to the measure of stopping the trade, a measure pregnant with injury to both parties, with an immediate loss of revenue to the local government, and with the great commercial and financial embarrassment to the East India Company, should it fail of success. The very desperation of the measure required the utmost firmness in carrying it into effect, and in this the supercargoes were not wanting. A regular negotiation upon the points at issue was allowed by the Viceroy. Mandarines of rank were appointed to meet Sir George Staunton (deputed from the Select Committee for that purpose) on a footing of equality, and the result was the removal and satisfactory explanation of the subject of complaint."—Vol. i. p. 69.

In order, however, to give an adequate idea of the difficulties which were encountered, and the value of ultimate success, it is proper to add that I was compelled at one time to break off the negotiation, to strike the British flag, and to retire with the whole body of British subjects from Canton; and that it was only when our ships were upon the point of sailing through the Bocca Tigris, and thus finally quitting the port, that I was overtaken by such a conciliatory overture from the Viceroy as warranted me in returning to Canton and renewing the negotiation.

It was not to be supposed that such a victory over the Chinese constituted authorities, though won by the employment of no other weapons than merely those of argument and an appeal to the universal principles of justice, forcibly addressed to the Chinese in their native language, though in a spirit of British independence, could easily be forgiven. Complaints against me, *individually*, were transmitted by the local officers, both publicly and secretly, to the Court of Pekin; and a special order was obtained from the Emperor, authorising the Viceroy to adopt extreme measures against me, if it should appear expedient. Fortunately, however, for me, the high spirit which then prevailed throughout the British community in China was too well known by the mandarines, to allow them to venture on any measures of outrage or violence, and I was never in any manner molested.

During the short period in which I held the chief direction of our commercial affairs in China, I had little more to do than to provide that the British interests sustained no actual injury or degradation under my guardianship. I had certainly, in the earlier periods of my career in China, fondly anticipated that I might have signalised my chiefship with some great changes and large reforms. Some few improvements I did make in the system, but much of what I had

imagined to have been *abuses*, I found to
have been the indispensable and practical
adaptation of the old system to new circumstances. The chief error which it appeared to me requisite to correct, was a
certain degree of latitude in the mode of
recording our transactions, which opened a
door, however unjustly, to suspicion. It was
impossible for any man to exceed in honour
or integrity my predecessor, Mr. Elphinstone;
but I held it to be necessary, not only to do
right abstractedly, but also to guard against
misconstruction, and to avoid even the appearance of evil.

I now come to the period of my connexion with the mission of Lord Amherst
to China. This measure did not at all
originate with me or my friends. The moment was not in our opinions favourable.
The arrangements were in several respects
also concluded in opposition to the advice
and opinion of my friend, Sir John Barrow,
the individual decidedly best informed on

the subject.   It was sent out for the single
purpose of settling the Canton disputes and
re-establishing the trade; but these objects
had been completely effected previous to its
arrival in China.   Our chief solicitude, therefore, was so to provide, that a scheme which
had been injudicious in its plan, and superfluous as to its object, should not do harm
to the cause which it had been sent out
to promote; and, at all events, not to re-
cede from that high and honourable position
which our commercial representatives had
taken at Canton, as well as our former
diplomatic representative, Lord Macartney,
had taken at Pekin.

Notwithstanding these discouragements
to any very sanguine expectations of success,
I took the deepest interest, both from duty
and from feeling, in all the proceedings of
this Embassy, from its commencement to its
close.   The records of our establishment for
the first six months of the year 1816, bear
testimony to my frequent and anxious devo-
tion to all the preparatory measures; and,

during the remaining six months of that
year, my colleagues and companions on the
Embassy will bear witness that my position
in it was no sinecure. In fact, during those
six months we maintained a constant intercourse with the officers of the Chinese government in the interior of the Chinese empire,
and in the face of the whole Chinese population. Except in the instance of Lord Macartney's Embassy, in 1792, no British subject had ever penetrated into these regions,
and the British name was as yet little known,
and still less esteemed. I think it must be
obvious to every reflecting individual, that,
under such very singular circumstances, the
mere ceremonials of a court reception, had
they taken place, would have been nothing
compared to the moral effect which the judiciously sustained proceedings of the British
Mission would be calculated to produce.

Thus, although this mission has often
been stigmatised as a failure, it was practically, perhaps, the most successful of any
that had ever been sent to Pekin by any

European power; for it was followed by a longer interval of commercial tranquillity, and of freedom from annoyance, than had ever been experienced before. See "Davis's China," Vol. i. p. 104.

The peculiar degree of responsibility which was thrown upon me, in consequence of Lord Amherst and Mr. Ellis, my two colleagues in the Commission, preferring to act upon my opinion rather than their own, with respect to the decisive question of the *Kotou*, or Chinese ceremony, is well known. It was the more gratifying to me, under the pressure of such responsibility, to receive from Lord Amherst, five years after the event, a letter, containing the following assurance:—

"I have never for a moment regretted that I suffered myself to be guided by your opinion. It is impossible that even *you* should feel more gratified than I do at the complete fulfilment of all your predictions."

Mr. Ellis expresses himself in his published narrative nearly in similar terms:—

"I do not in the least blame myself for having

surrendered my opinion to the experience of Sir George Staunton. It is difficult for persons arguing from general principles to appreciate the exact effects of impressions in a particular scene, that impression being probably made up of circumstances with which they are unacquainted, or to which they do not assign their proper importance. The only safe course, therefore, on such an occasion is to defer to local experience."—Vol. i. p. 233.

The kind feelings expressed by Mr. Ellis towards me personally, in the following passage, are too flattering and gratifying to me to be omitted :—

"At three o'clock we reached the Alceste, where we had a parting dinner with Sir George Staunton, who goes to England in the Scaleby Castle. He carries with him the good wishes of all the party, and, though the acquaintance of those who came from England in the Alceste has been shorter, I question if they yield in esteem to his older friends at Canton. For my own part, while I, perhaps unfortunately, retained my original opinion respecting the Tartar ceremony, I must confess that I could not have found another person to whose character and acquirements I would have preferred yielding the guidance of my actions."—Vol. ii. p. 195.

The opinions which were entertained of
my conduct in the Embassy by those *older*
friends, to whom Mr. Ellis alludes, will appear from the following letter, which was
transmitted to me from China, about three
years after my return to England, and is
signed by sixteen members of the British
Factory at Canton, including the six gentlemen who successively filled the office of
Chief, between the period of my retirement,
in 1817, and the abolition of the establishment, in 1834; the last of whom, Sir John
Davis, Baronet, is now Her Majesty's Plenipotentiary in China, and Governor of Hong
Kong.

" To Sir George Thomas Staunton, Baronet.
" Sir,
        " We, the undersigned members of the
British Factory in China, fully appreciating the
extent and merit of your services when a Commissioner of Embassy to this country, request your
acceptance of the accompanying testimonial of the
high estimation in which we hold the principles
which governed your conduct.
        " The decision and sound judgment displayed

by you under circumstances the most trying, when less firm minds might have bent under the weight of the responsibility you incurred, maintained our national honour, while they have promoted our commercial interests; and these must ever have a necessary and an intimate connexion.

" We feel satisfied that every man whom experience has made acquainted with the nature and constitution of the government of China, must entertain a similar opinion; and it is to us a source of pleasing reflection that, while the interests of the great and valuable commerce confided to your care were by you ably upheld, our character, as the subjects of a free and independent state, has remained unsullied and entire.

" We request you will receive this as the expression of our deliberate opinion, and, with best wishes for your health and happiness,

" We remain your sincere and faithful friends,

(Signed)

JAS. B. URMSTON.	JOHN JACKSON.
W. FRASER.	TH. C. SMITH.
W. BOSANQUET.	J. LIVINGSTONE.
W. H. C. PLOWDEN.	R. MORRISON.
CHAS. MILLETT.	S. BALL.
C. MARJORIBANKS.	J. REEVES.
J. F. DAVIS.	F. H. TOONE.
A. PEARSON.	T. J. METCALFE.

The above letter was accompanied by a splendid silver-gilt salver, valued at six hundred guineas.

After such testimonies in favour of the course of policy which I had recommended, it seems almost superfluous to add any other; but as a writer in the " Edinburgh Review," in his notice of Mr. Ellis's Narrative, takes the opposite view of the subject, it may not be immaterial to observe that every other reviewer (without exception, as far as I know,) has advocated my side of the question. I subjoin a few extracts.

Monthly Review.

" To have added encouragement to their insolence, therefore, could not have been good policy; and we are convinced that the motives which influenced Sir George Staunton in his advice to the Ambassador were sound and statesmanlike." — P. 9.

British Critic.

" To talk of keeping up relations between the Court of London and such a court as that of Pekin, is manifestly idle; and we are very doubtful whether any more effectual method could have been hit upon of impressing the Chinese people with a conviction of the power and dignity of this country than that followed by Lord Amherst."— P. 601.

British Review.

" Now, we cannot conceal our astonishment that, after knowing the facts connected with the Dutch Embassy in 1794, Mr. Ellis should have hesitated one moment as to the expediency of refusing most peremptorily to make the *Kotou*."—P. 148.

Eclectic Review.

" Sir George Staunton, incomparably, and in every point of view, the best judge, steadily counselled resistance."

Dr. Morrison's Memoir of the Embassy.

" She (Great Britain) still wisely refuses to perform by her Ambassador that ceremony which is the expression of homage."—P. 142.

My career of public service abroad terminated with Lord Amherst's Embassy. Having held the highest place in that branch of the service of the East India Company to which I was attached; having accomplished

my favourite object, of revisiting Pekin in a
diplomatic capacity; and, having accumulated
a competent fortune in addition to my patrimonial inheritance, I gladly abandoned the
prospect of increased wealth, which the cus-
tomary period of a five years' residence
would have afforded me; and I rejoiced to
find myself able to terminate the period of
my banishment, at the early age of six-
and-thirty.

I landed in England in June 1817; and
if my services to the public at home in
connexion with our interests in China, during
the long interval of more than twenty-eight
years, which have elapsed since that period,
have not been so frequent or continuous as
might have been expected from the nature of
my previous habits and employments, it has
not been my fault. I repeatedly offered my
services to the Government, as an unsalaried
member of the India Board, which was, in
fact, the only official station in which my services connected with China were available;

and although my offers were declined, I always readily gave my assistance, privately, when applied to (as frequently occurred), both by the President of that Board, and other members of the Government. I insert here the following letter from Mr. Grant, when President of the India Board (now Lord Glenelg), to show that, whatever the motives may have been for declining to accept of my services *officially*, the refusal did not proceed either from a low estimation of those services, or the exclusion, as alleged, of all China affairs from the Board's jurisdiction.

" *India Board, December* 13*th*, 1831.

" My dear Sir,

" I venture to address you confidentially on the subject of our relations with China. You are of course aware of the recent transactions at Canton, and I am very anxious to know your view as to the line of conduct which the Government ought to pursue. It would oblige me extremely if you would favour me with your opinion. I trust you will pardon my troubling you, the importance of the occasion, and the public interests involved in the question, will, I am persuaded, form in your mind the best apology for this intrusion.

" I am, &c., &c.,

(Signed)   " CHARLES GRANT.

" Sir George Staunton, Bart. M.P."

My time did not, however, hang heavy on my hands during this period. I published a curious translation of the Embassy of the Emperor Kang-Hee to the Tourgouth Tartars, in 1712; which was very well received, and is long since out of print; and also a volume of Miscellaneous Notices of China, which arrived at a second edition. I printed, likewise, for private circulation amongst my friends, a second volume of Miscellaneous Notices on China, a volume of my father's Memoirs and Family History, and a detailed Narrative of the Proceedings of Lord Amherst's Embassy.

No opportunity of free election being as yet open to me, I sat in the House of Commons, between the years 1818 and 1833, for the close boroughs of St. Michael's, in Cornwall, and Heytesbury, in Wiltshire.

I was examined, at this period, at considerable length upon China affairs, by the Committees of the Two Houses; and, when I was named a Member of the East India Committee of the House of Commons, in 1830, a fair field seemed at length opened to me for endeavouring to render the knowledge and experience I possessed on China affairs serviceable to the public. It is true, on the other hand, that neither my habits nor my education had well qualified me for the warfare of public discussion, especially when subject to the disadvantage of having to act in opposition to the current of public feeling, which, at that time, ran strongly against the East India Company, and in favour of large and precipitate changes in our Oriental commerce. I did not, nevertheless, shrink from the task which I conceived to have been imposed upon me; and I determined to place at least on record, those principles, of the truth of which I felt convinced, and the neglect of which, our statesmen and legislators, I knew would, a few years after, greatly and unanimously regret.

My first step was to move in the East India Committee for certain papers, which were necessary to establish my case. Even this preliminary motion was strongly contested, and only carried by rather a close division in the Committee, at the end of two days' debate. My next step was to move in the House of Commons a series of Resolutions, grounded upon the official documents that I had obtained in the Committee. If these Resolutions had been carried, they would have warranted me in proposing to the House, thirdly, certain modifications in the new charter of the East India Company, which would have rendered the transition from Exclusive to Free Trade, less precipitate and perilous; and which, to say the least, would (as already stated) have averted the unfortunate catastrophe of the expulsion and death of Lord Napier.

Twice I obtained, in the usual routine of business, a favourable opportunity for

bringing the question before the House, and
each time I consented to relinquish my opportunity, at the instance of the Government, on the plea of public inconvenience.
When I did at length bring the question
forward, the moment happened to be peculiarly unfavourable. The House was thin,
and, having been counted out, I could not
even bring the Resolutions to a vote, which
was essential to their being placed upon
record. They were finally moved by me, on
the 13th of June, 1833, by way of amendment to the motion of the President of the
India Board, to go into Committee upon the
renewal of the charter, but an understanding
was come to, that they were to be negatived
without debate or division.

I must here suspend my narrative for a
moment, in order to quote the terms in
which these same Resolutions were appealed
to, with praise, *seven years after*, by both
sides of the House. In the debate upon
the China war, in April 1840, Sir James

Graham, a member of Sir Robert Peel's
Cabinet, spoke as follows : —

"It is impossible for me to refer to any authority more entitled to weight and respect than
that of the Hon. member for Portsmouth (Sir
George Staunton). Wisdom, *après coup*, is of
very little value, but that foresight which anti-
cipates the future must be regarded with admiration, when subsequent events come to be considered. Sir George Staunton, before the China
Trade Act was introduced, took occasion to move
certain Resolutions. They now stand upon the
Journals of the House as a memorial of his sagacity, of his knowledge, and of the wisdom which
dictated them." — *Minutes of Parliament*, p. 2388.

Mr. Charles Buller, a leading member of
the Opposition, gave a similar testimony. He
said : —

" As to 'prospective foresight,' the only person
who had manifested it was the Hon. Member for
Portsmouth (Sir George Staunton), and I refer
to the circumstance with great regret and humiliation, who proposed the six Resolutions relative to the new system of trade, to which the
Right Honourable Baronet has adverted."—P.2449.

I must say, in justice to the President of the India Board, Mr. Grant, that, although he decidedly opposed my Resolutions, and little anticipated the meed of approbation they were destined to receive from both sides of the House seven years after, he treated me with great consideration and courtesy.

He observed,—

" I am sorry to say that I altogether differ from my Honourable friend upon these points. I do so with the most unfeigned diffidence, because, upon a subject of this kind, I am aware that he is an authority entitled to the highest respect. Considering the extent to which my Honourable friend has carried his acquaintance with the language, the manners, the feelings, and the habits of thinking, of the Chinese, I repeat that it is with the most unfeigned diffidence, and with no small difficulty, that I venture to offer an opinion in opposition to his, upon points so nearly connected with the character of that people."

I will not here enter into the *arguments* on either side, but merely ask the question (in reference to the fate of Lord Napier), which of us was the truest prophet ?

G

Paragraph of Sir George Staunton's Resolutions.

" Without the previous sanction of a national treaty, any attempt to appoint national functionaries at Canton for the protection of Trade, will, in the present state of our relations with China, not only prove of little advantage to the subject, but be liable, in a serious degree, to compromise the honour and dignity of the Crown."

Mr. Grant's Reply.

" I think that if we do not ourselves sound the note of alarm, the Chinese will receive any functionary whom we may appoint as the representative of the British nation at Canton without any of the suspicion and distrust which the formal process of a negotiation would be sure to awaken in the minds of a people so sensitive and so jealous; and that the ordinary transactions of business between them and us would proceed with little or no interruption."

Instead of receiving our representative " without suspicion or distrust," as Mr. Grant had expected, it will be painfully remembered that they expelled him so rudely and abruptly, as actually to occasion his death!

In the following year (1834) I became

a member of the Committee of the House of Commons on the Tea Duties; and I supported by a speech in the House, as well as by my regular attendance in the Committee, the plan of a uniform duty, in preference to a graduated scale. The Government carried the latter in the Committee by one vote; but they were compelled to abandon it in the following year, my predictions of its inconvenience and liability to fraud having been fully verified.

When it was supposed that the interruption of the Trade on the death of Lord Napier would render another mission to Pekin necessary, I submitted to the consideration of the Government, that although I did not venture to recommend a mission to Pekin, I was willing, in the event of it having been decided upon, to undertake it, and to do my best to ensure its success. All who knew me, and my position and health, at that period, will give me credit for having made a very *disinterested* offer;

and will congratulate me upon it *not* having
been accepted.

In 1836, when an attempt was made, in
pamphlets published by Mr. Lindsay, Mr.
Matheson, and others, to excite the public
mind in favour of hostilities with China, on
grounds which appeared to me wholly un-
tenable, and with means which appeared to
me ridiculously inadequate, I thought it
my duty to take up my pen in the cause
of peace. The Athenæum weekly paper
noticed my pamphlet as follows:—

" The little tract by Sir George Staunton is
by far the most able we have seen on the subject
of our present relations with China. The writer
takes a sober, statesmanlike view of the question,
and, if it may be permitted to us, without pre-
sumption, to say so, enforces the opinions we
lately expressed with all the weight of one speaking from experience."

The pamphlet was on the whole well received, and carried to a second edition. If I
in any degree contributed on this occasion to
arrest the conflict until the unprovoked out-

rages of the Chinese had placed the right on *our* side, and justified as well as enabled us to put forth the strength of this great empire in the cause, I certainly wrote to good purpose.

In 1838 Lord Palmerston brought a Bill into the House of Commons under the title of the China Courts Bill. Although the objects proposed to be attained by this Bill were extremely desirable in themselves, it appeared to me altogether objectionable in the actual state of our relations with China. The papers laid before Parliament in support of the Bill did not at all remove my objections, and I communicated my opinions privately to this effect to Lord Palmerston; but his Lordship, having determined to persevere with the Bill, I had no other course but to give notice of my objections in the shape of an amendment to the second reading.

The discussion on the Bill did not come on till the latter end of July, after my usual period for leaving London; but Mr. Hawes, the member for Lambeth, took up the question for me, and, having moved my amendments, the Bill, after considerable debate, was withdrawn.

In the spring of the following year the violent and treacherous proceedings of the Canton authorities produced a rupture with China, and were followed by a series of hostile operations on our part against the Chinese, for the purpose of obtaining reparation for the injuries that had been inflicted upon our merchants, and an adequate guarantee for the peaceful prosecution of our commerce for the future. Our first measures were feeble and injudicious; but the necessity, and indeed humanity, of hastening the conclusion of the contest by more vigorous exertions, was at length felt; and, at the end of a third campaign, the war was happily terminated by the Treaty of Nanking, in August 1842; which not only secured for this country the reparation and guarantee which had been originally demanded, but placed our relations with China generally upon an enlarged and highly satisfactory basis.

I can neither charge myself with censure, nor take any credit, for the opening measures adopted by the Government. I was not consulted till the month of February: but, in the debate on the China war, on the occasion of Sir James Graham's motion, in April 1840, I took an active, and, I have reason to believe, effectual part in vindicating the Government policy, which appeared to me to have been opposed solely on party grounds. It was afterwards carried out with vigour, and to the fullest extent, by its most strenuous opponents, the moment they came into power. I considered the Government to blame in respect to Lord Napier's appointment; and I also totally dissented from the policy of the East India Company and the Legislature in respect to the Opium Trade; but, that neutral policy having been adopted, all the Government could do was to guard their representative in China from committing the country by the direct sanction of the opium trade, and authorising him, within such limits, to use his discretion. This they certainly did; and it was therefore unjust to blame them for not giving him (Captain Elliot) more explicit instructions, and equally absurd to hold them responsible for a contingency which no previous acts of the Chinese had rendered probable, and which no precaution in China, or instructions from home, could have averted.

The following extracts from Lord Palmerston's notes to me will sufficiently show the extent of my share in these transactions:—

1.

" 5 *Carlton Terrace*, 16*th February*, 1840.

" My dear Staunton,

"I should like very much to have your opinion upon a point or two connected with these China matters. Could you without inconvenience call on me this afternoon, at any time between half past four and six.

" Yours sincerely,
(Signed)   " PALMERSTON.
" Sir George Staunton, Bart."

2.

" *Carlton Terrace,* 19*th February,* 1840.

" My dear Staunton,

" I am very much obliged to you for your very interesting and valuable letter, of which you shall have a copy returned you.

" Yours sincerely,
(Signed) " PALMERSTON.
" Sir George Staunton, Bart."

3.

" *Carlton Terrace,* 2*d April,* 1840.

" My dear Staunton,

" I looked for you last night in the House of Commons, but you had, I fancy, gone home before I arrived. I wished to have had five minutes' talk with you about China. I will take my chance of finding you at home at half-past twelve to-day.

" Yours sincerely,
(Signed) " PALMERSTON.
" Sir George Staunton, Bart."

4.

" *Carlton Terrace,* 8*th April,* 1840.

" My dear Staunton,

" You must allow me to thank you for

your excellent and very effective speech, which
made a great impression on the House.

"Yours sincerely,

(Signed) "PALMERSTON."

5.

"*Foreign Office, 29th of May,* 1841.

"My dear Staunton,

"I should be very glad if you could allow
Sir Henry Pottinger to have half-an-hour's conversation with you before he starts, which he will
do on Monday. If there is any hour to-morrow
at which you could receive him, he would call
upon you ; and if you should be able to receive
him, perhaps you would write him a line to say
so. His direction is 36 Berkeley Square.

"Yours sincerely,

(Signed) "PALMERSTON.

"Sir George Staunton, Bart."

6.

"*Carlton Terrace, 1st June,* 1841.

"My dear Staunton,

"Thank you much for your note, and for
seeing Pottinger.

"Pray do give us a word to-morrow evening
about Chinese affairs. It would be of great use
to us, and it would come in well after the news

of to-day, which, however, I have no account of,
as yet.

"Yours sincerely,

(Signed) "PALMERSTON.

"Sir George Staunton, Bart."

In March 1842, I moved for certain
papers connected with the claims of the
British merchants for compensation for the
opium surrenderȩd to the Chinese authorities; and, a few days after, I seconded Mr.
Lindsay's motion in favour of those claims,
in a speech of some length. I did so, con-
ceiving that, although the Opium Trade
could not be too strongly reprobated, it
had been carried on with the knowledge
and sanction of the British Government,
and that, consequently, the claims of the
merchants for compensation for property
taken from them, under such circumstances,
with illegal violence, were perfectly valid.

The following letter from the Earl of
Aberdeen, who succeeded Lord Palmerston in
the Foreign Office, will show that the change
of ministry did not preclude me from entering

into confidential communications on Chinese
matters with the Government:—

"(*Private*)   *Foreign Office, Dec.* 12*th*, 1842.
    " Dear Sir,
        " I have to thank you for the extract of the
letter from one of the Interpreters attached to the
Mission in China, which you had the goodness to
send me, and which, I entirely agree with you in
thinking, deserves the best attention of the Government.
    " I hope I need not say that, on the interesting
and important subject of our future relations with
China, I shall be most happy to receive any sug-
gestions or information with which you may think
proper to furnish me.
    " In a matter of so much difficulty and uncer-
tainty it would be great arrogance to reject
assistance from any quarter, but it would be
unpardonable to do so from a person so well
entitled to attention as yourself.
        " I am, dear Sir, very truly yours,
                (Signed)   " ABERDEEN.
    " Sir Geo. T. Staunton, Bart."

In April 1843, I spoke at considerable
length in the House in support of Lord

Ashley's Motion against the Opium Trade, and I afterwards published my speech. I did not take up the question (as Lord Ashley did) exclusively on the *moral* ground, but argued it more especially on the ground that any sanction or countenance of such a contraband trade with China, was wholly inconsistent with our treaty of peace and amity with that Empire, and, therefore, likely in a short period to occasion another rupture. The Chinese government having, however, since practically (although without any specific enactment) legalised this traffic, the international argument against it, of course, falls to the ground.

When it became generally known that Sir Henry Pottinger had applied to be relieved, and that a successor was about to be appointed, I felt so strong a conviction of the mischief which must ensue from the selection of a prejudiced or incompetent person for the supreme direction of our affairs in China at this critical period, that I ventured to submit to Lord Aberdeen my persuasion that Mr. John Francis Davis, who had formerly held successively the offices of Chief under the Company and Plenipotentiary under the Crown, was the most qualified individual that could be chosen to succeed Sir Henry Pottinger.

I very shortly received from Lord Aberdeen the following courteous reply:—

"(*Private*)   *Foreign Office, December* 21*st*, 1843.

"My dear Sir,

"You could not have more fully complied with the spirit of my invitation, or have given me more useful and important information, than you have done by your note of the day before yesterday.

"I am unable at this moment to give any distinct pledge on the subject, further than to assure you that it shall receive the best consideration. I also beg to offer you my sincere thanks for your note.

"Very sincerely yours,

(Signed)   "ABERDEEN.

"Sir George T. Staunton, Bart."

Four days after the date of the above letter, Mr. Davis was sent for, and offered the appointment. Finding, however, afterwards that Mr. Davis had declined to proceed to China, in consequence of Sir Robert Peel having objected to propose to the Queen to confer upon him a Baronetcy, which he conceived to be essential in order to give him due weight in his new office, I requested a personal interview with Lord Aberdeen upon the subject, and had the satisfaction to receive authority from his Lordship to convey to Mr. Davis the assurance of the Government that the Patent of dignity of a Baronet would be sent out to him a few months after his departure. This assurance removed his objections, and, on the 17th of January, 1844, he finally accepted the appointment. On the 1st of March he embarked for China.

On the 26th of March I moved for an address to the Crown in favour of a provision for the family of the late Rev. Dr. Morrison. I transcribe the following complimentary para-

graph on the subject, which appeared in some
of the newspapers, on the occasion :—

"In the advocacy of a claim which had so
properly devolved upon one of the most profound
of living Orientalists whom Europe can boast,
Sir George Staunton delivered himself with that
habitual modesty which has won for him the
respect of all parties. He alone seemed to be
unconscious of the authority with which he must
be speaking on such a question in the House of
Commons, in reference to his own long residence
in a portion of the Chinese Empire, to his extraordinary proficiency in the Chinese language, and
to that peculiar knowledge of the Chinese people
and the policy of their government, which he had
evinced under the most trying circumstances that
could test his judgment, or tax his discretion."

The same writer afterwards notices Sir
Robert Peel's reply with caustic severity.
He says,—

"Sir Robert Peel resisted the motion for an
address to the Crown with every minute micro-
scopic atom of an objection which he could detect
amidst the worthless dust of his official depositories."

The motion was, of course, withdrawn:

but I received, a very few days after, an autograph note from Sir Robert Peel to the following effect:—

"*Whitehall, March* 30*th*, 1844.

"Sir Robert Peel presents his compliments to Sir George Staunton, and has the satisfaction of acquainting him that Sir Robert Peel has made arrangements by which an additional one hundred pounds per annum will be secured to the relatives of the late Mr. Morrison, and he proposes to appropriate this sum in the following manner:— twenty-five pounds to Mrs. Pearce, and seventy-five pounds to Mrs. Morrison. Sir Robert Peel regrets that he cannot hold out the expectation of further aid to the family of the late Dr. Morrison."

This decision was satisfactory, as far as it went; and if I could have obtained a further sum of fifty pounds annually for each of the four surviving children of Dr. Morrison by his second marriage, I should have thought that I had done as much as, under all circumstances, could have been fairly expected. I could not, however, rest

H

satisfied with this one-sided provision for a *part only* of the family, and I therefore ventured to press this subject again on Sir Robert Peel, first by letter, and then by a motion for papers connected with the late Mr. Morrison's services. These papers were granted me, Sir Robert Peel having consented to their production, on the understanding that he was not thereby pledged to anything farther.

Upon the authority of these papers, I gave notice of a second motion, which was the only chance, though a slender one, of doing something more for the family. At all events, it would have given me an opportunity of replying to some of the objections of Sir Robert Peel, which I had not been prepared to do at the moment they were made. Mr. Hankey, however, on behalf of the family, and supported by the advice of Mr. Mangles, M.P., interposed to request of me to postpone my motion till the return to England of Sir Henry Pottinger. I, of course, submitted to such

authority, though contrary to my own opinion, and I was thus released from the duty
of the further prosecution of what had become
a very irksome suit. The result was, as I
expected, fatal to the claim; for Sir Henry
Pottinger declined to take it up, and it is
now utterly beyond the reach of revival by
any one else.

In the course of the year 1845 I have
had the gratification of rendering some service, to my friend, Mr. (now Sir John) Davis:
first, by defending him in the House of Commons against a vexatious attack on some of
his Hong Kong ordinances; and, secondly,
by pressing on Her Majesty's Government
the fulfilment of their promise to confer upon
him a Baronetcy. I flatter myself that my
speech had a considerable effect in preventing
the motion from receiving support in the
House; and, with respect to the Baronetcy,
although I fully acquit Her Majesty's Government of any settled intention to evade
their engagements, I cannot but think that

my letter to Sir Robert Peel contributed something to the *promptitude* of their fulfilment.

Sir John Davis has very handsomely acknowledged these services in his recent letters to me, of which the following are extracts:—

> "*Hong Kong, May* 29*th*, 1845.
>
> "It was very kind of you to take my part against the Hong Kong Ordinances. A word from your side of the House is worth *two* from the other to a Government man; and the event proved this, by his finding no supporters to his motion."

> "*Hong Kong, September* 13*th*, 1845.
>
> "I am extremely obliged to you for the cogent letter you wrote to Sir Robert Peel, and am persuaded that, whenever the promotion comes, it will be owing in a very large measure to yourself.
>
> "*September* 26*th*.—Since the foregoing was written, I have had the pleasure to receive yours of the 15th July, announcing my title. I can assure you I consider it has come, in a great measure, from yourself, without whose exertions I might still have been without it.
>
> (Signed)   "J. F. Davis.
>
> "Sir George Staunton, Bart."

At the risk of some repetition, the following may be perhaps more full.

It remains for me to give some account of my literary pursuits connected with China since my final retirement from my station in that country. I have not on this subject a great deal to say. My Chinese *studies*, strictly so termed, I dropped at once and for ever, to use an expression of Sir William Jones, " deep as plummet ever sounded," immediately upon my final embarkation for Europe. I have never possessed in this country the leisure, the means, or the inducement, to revert to my Chinese literary pursuits. By the phrase I allude to the assistance of native scholars, without which (except in the extraordinary instance of the profoundly learned and indefatigable Mons. Stanislas Julien, of Paris) I suspect no important translations from the Chinese by Europeans have ever been successfully made. But, although I have added nothing to my stock of translation from the Chinese since my return to this country, I have had some

occupation in arranging and preparing for
the press those which I had previously
written, and brought home with me; and
also in accompanying them with prefaces,
notes, and commentaries. I have printed
altogether, since my return, five octavo volumes, and four or five pamphlets; but only
two of the *former* and *two* of the *latter* were
published for sale. The others were printed
for private circulation amongst friends.

The first of these volumes was published
in 1821, and entitled, " Narrative of the
Chinese Embassy to the Khan of the Tourgouth Tartars," translated from the original
Chinese, and accompanied by an Appendix
of Miscellaneous Translations. This volume
was as favourably received as the larger
work of the " Chinese Penal Code," published
eleven years before. Although intrinsically
of less importance, it was more popular as
a book for general reading, and has long
since been out of print. The following are
extracts from the remarks upon it of some
of the Reviewers :—

British Critic.

" The translations which Sir George Staunton
has now presented to the public are eminently
valuable, as closer portraits of manners than any
with which we hitherto have met; and as afford-
ing us, for the first time, some key to the policy
which guides this vast Empire in its external
relations. Of the fidelity of Sir George Staunton's translations we cannot pretend to judge,
but his high character, both as an individual
and a scholar, may be received as a sufficient
pledge. This volume, perhaps, contains more
which will gratify the curiosity of an inquirer
than give amusement to a mere light reader;
but the style of his versions is easy, flowing, and
natural. We are indebted to him for an addition
to a branch of literature, which few are competent
to increase, and with which none have shown
themselves more profoundly or more usefully acquainted than himself."—Pp. 418-427.

Eclectic Review.

" The volume now before us illustrates their
foreign relations; but the *Embassy* yields considerably in point of interest to the other contents
of the volume, which Sir George has subjoined in
the form of an Appendix. We have consulted an
authority which is decisive with us on all subjects

of this nature, and we learn from that source that the versions are close and accurate, and faithful transcripts of the sense and diction of the original."
—P. 43.

Blackwood's Magazine.

"In taking our leave of this singular and interesting book, which certainly brings us better acquainted with the Chinese people and government than any other work which we have ever perused, it would be injustice to the translator to forbear noticing the very able manner in which he appears to have surmounted the various and great difficulties of his undertaking. We cannot, indeed, from our own knowledge speak with certainty as to the accuracy with which the original is rendered, but the whole is written with so much simplicity, perspicuity, and elegance, and exhibits such internal evidence of fidelity, that even were the rare acquirements of Sir George Staunton, and the soundness of his understanding, less known to us, we should feel little hesitation in recommending it to the attention of our readers, not only as one of the most curious literary productions of the age, but also as a faithful and highly intelligent version of the original Chinese narrative."—P. 221.

In 1822 I published another octavo volume under the title of " Miscellaneous Notices relating to China, and our Commercial Intercourse with that Country." This work arrived at a second edition, but did not attract much notice from the Reviewers, either in the shape of praise or censure. In fact, the purely *literary* portion of it was rather scanty; and the *commercial* portion consisted chiefly of a defence of opinions which were not at that time generally popular.

The three volumes which I subsequently printed for private circulation amongst my friends were entitled, " Miscellaneous Notices relating to China, Part the Second." " Notes of Proceedings and Occurrences during the British Embassy to Pekin, in 1816;" and " Memoir of the Life and Family of the late Sir George Leonard Staunton, Bart., with an Appendix, consisting of Illustrations and Authorities, and a Copious Selection from his Private Correspondence." Not more than from seventy to two hundred copies of these works having been printed, and those only circulated *privately,* they could not, of course, come under the notice of the Reviewers; but I cannot refuse myself the pleasure of inserting the private letters of thanks for copies of the Memoir of my father's life, which I received from the Marquis of Lansdowne, the Duke of Rutland, and the late Dr. Gillies, the learned historian of Greece.

"*Berkeley Square, April* 21*st,* 1823.

"Dear Sir George,

"I request you will accept my sincere thanks for your obliging note, and the volume which accompanied it.

"If anything could add in my mind to the interest it must excite in all those to whom the personal merit, literary character, and public services, of the late Sir George Staunton are known, it would be his long acquaintance with my father, who always, I know, entertained for him the sincerest respect and regard. I have the honour to be, dear Sir George,

"Your very faithful servant,
(Signed) "LANSDOWNE.

"Sir George Staunton, Bart."

" *Cheveley Park, April* 29*th,* 1823.

" Sir,

" I have to acknowledge, with many thanks, your note of the 19th ultimo, accompanied by a volume, containing the history of your family.

" It would have been interesting to me under any circumstances, but it is particularly so, as containing facts of much importance, in which the early history of my own family claim a share. The work which you have been kind enough to send me reached me only on Saturday last, or it would have experienced an earlier acknowledgment. I am proud to recollect the fact which you mention, of our having been contemporaries for a short time, at Trinity College, Cambridge. I have the honour to be, Sir,

" Your most obedient and faithful servant,

(Signed) " RUTLAND.

" Sir George Staunton, Bart."

" 9 *Upper Seymour Street, April* 22*d,* 1823.

" Dear Sir George,

" I felt honoured and gratified in no common degree by the present of your Memoir of your father's life : a work which I have perused with avidity, and found highly interesting, from the nature of the subject, and from the delightful manner in which it is treated. Having been several

years an associate of your father's in the Athenian
Club, I had an opportunity of admiring and loving
him for his head and heart; and his conversations,
and many instances of his good-will and friendship,
have been ever present in my memory. Believe
me, dear Sir George, with the greatest regard,
"Your obliged and faithful servant,
(Signed) "JOHN GILLIES.
"Sir George Staunton, Bart."

With respect to the pamphlets which I
have printed at different times, it will be
sufficient to record here their titles:—

All the most prominent circumstances of my Parliamentary life connected with *China* have now been told. I first came into Parliament at the general election, in 1818, as one of the members for the borough of St. Michael's, or Midshall, in Cornwall. Having, in the course of the preceding year, retired from the public service abroad, and not finding any official employment in the line of my former pursuits open to me at home, it naturally became an object of my ambition to obtain access to those interesting and honourable employments which are the consequence of a seat in Parliament. I did not at that time possess either landed property or parliamentary connexions of any kind in *England;* and, although my family had, in former times, possessed considerable parliamentary influence in the county of Galway, in *Ireland,* and several individuals of the family had successively represented the town or county in the Irish Parliament, it was out of the question for me, as an *Englishman,* resident in *England,* to attempt to revive that influence. A close borough was accordingly my only resource. A seat for St. Michael's having been placed at my option on terms of perfect independence, I gladly accepted it.

From the first day that I took my seat in the House of Commons, in January 1819, down to the present hour (January 1852), I have sided with that section of our great political parties which, previous to 1830, were usually denominated the " Liberal Tories," who acknowledged Mr. Canning as their leader; and who, soon after his death, seceded from the Tories of Lord Liverpool's school, and became amalgamated with the Whigs. *With them*, I gave a general and independent *support* to Lord Liverpool's administration. *With them*, I invariably *opposed* Lord Liverpool and the ultra - Tories upon the Catholic question. *With them*, I finally and entirely separated from that party, on the occasion of the Duke of Wellington's celebrated declaration of unqualified opposition to all Parliamentary Re-

form. *With them*, lastly, I have ever since
given to the Liberal party a free and independent support. I am not pretending (but,
on the contrary, should have been *ashamed of
it* if it had been so,) that my political conduct
has been uninfluenced by the new circumstances in which our country has been placed
in from time to time, or that I have been indifferent to the new lights which have risen
from time to time above our political horizon,
and helped to disclose the true value and
bearings of public measures.

The sentiments were justly and truly expressed by the member for Oxfordshire, in
the year 1831 : —

"It was about that period that he had the
honour and the gratification of becoming acquainted
with the late Mr. Canning—one of the most con-
summate statesmen, and one of the most brilliant
orators, that had ever adorned the senate ; and
who, in the latter part of his life, had become a
most popular minister. From the moment in
which he perceived the powerful and zealous exertions which Mr. Canning made in the cause of
civil and religious liberty, he addicted himself

very much to the politics of that illustrious man. It was well known that Mr. Canning was an opponent of reform ; but from what he had seen and known of Mr. Canning, he thought it by no means unlikely that Mr. Canning, had he been spared to them until now, would have taken precisely the course which he (Mr. Harcourt) was then taking. Mr. Canning's main objection to reform was, that no proposition for reform in Parliament had ever yet been brought forward, which had received the sanction and assent of a large proportion of the people of this country. He thought there was much weight in this objection, and he confessed that if this objection were applicable to the bill of Lord John Russell, he should not have felt it his duty to support it. But the bill had been accepted by the reformers themselves as sufficient and satisfactory, and it had been hailed with almost unanimous approbation by the country at large. Thus, then, the main objection of Mr. Canning fell to the ground. Another argument urged by Mr. Canning was, that the representative system as it stood worked sufficiently well for all the purposes for which it was devised. He did not mean to say that in spite of those abuses which had prevented the operation of it being better, the system might not have worked well in former times, but now that the public attention had been

riveted upon those abuses,—now that the people
looked upon those abuses with disgust,—now that
they called for the immediate removal of them, and
now that the nation at large had made up their
minds that the system ought to be amended,—
under such circumstances, and with this condition
of public opinion, it was utterly impossible that
the system could work well for the time to come.
Yes, it was utterly impossible ; for no constitution,
no form of government, no system of policy, could
work well, which was not in harmony with the
disposition, and which had not the support, of the
majority of the people.   It had, however, been
said that great and clever men had been returned
to Parliament by means of rotten boroughs. This,
no doubt, was quite true.   It was as impossible to
deny that such men had so found their way into
Parliament, as it was to deny that such men had
been mixed with others of a very different description, whose absence might have been more
advantageous to the country than their presence,
and who, owing their seats to the same means as
the others, rendered the talents, and the virtues,
and genius, of the latter a dear purchase to the
country.   But suppose that the obtaining great
men by such means had been a good that more
than counterbalanced the evil.   It might have
been so in times past ; but it was impossible that

it could be so for the future. The eloquence of such men would now lose its charm, their reasoning would lose its attraction, and the weight that had formerly attached to their opinions would now, in the existing state of public feeling, be lost in the illegitimacy of their political birth. These arguments, then, which had formerly been urged by Mr. Canning were no longer applicable ; the circumstances of the present times had deprived them of whatever weight they might have had in times past. He thought he was justified, therefore, in saying that if Mr. Canning had survived until now, he believed that able and amiable man would have taken the course which he had made up his mind to pursue."—*Speech at Oxfordshire Election, May* 10, 1831.

I merely wish to show that my political course has not been an *insulated* or *capricious* one; but adopted in general unison with a large political party, which, all admit, includes within its ranks many disinterested and enlightened men. I had no kind of *interest* in opposing the Duke of Wellington's administration in November 1830 ; for, although that opposition may have, in some

degree, paved the way for my election by
the popular voice for South Hampshire, two
years after, I no more anticipated that event
at the time than I should have calculated on
becoming Prime Minister! So reluctant,
indeed, was I to give a vote against the
party with which I hitherto had acted, that
I hesitated to the last moment; and did not,
in point of fact, go out into the lobby until
I saw Sir Thomas Acland do so, of whose
honesty and independence I had conceived
a very high opinion. I have never received,
or desired to receive, the emoluments of office
under either party. I state this as a *fact*, not
as a *merit*, for if I had been a younger man,
and had been considered capable of office, I
should have been *proud* instead of ashamed
to serve my country for a fair pecuniary
reward, under an administration in the political views of which I generally concurred.

The death of George the Third, in January
1820, cut short the Parliament which had
been chosen in 1818; but I was re-elected
for St. Michael's in the general election

of April 1820, and sat for the second time
for that borough until the dissolution in
June 1826. Owing to the difference of
opinion which existed between me and the
patron of the borough, on the subject of the
Catholic Question, I was not again re-elected,
and remained out of Parliament till 1830,
when I was returned at the general election
for Heytesbury, in Wiltshire. I held my
seat for the close borough of Heytesbury
upon the same terms of perfect independence
as I had done my seat for St. Michael's; and,
when the Parliament was prematurely dissolved, after General Gascoigne's motion, in
April 1831, I was again returned for Heytesbury.

In the general election which ensued after
the passing of the Reform Bill, in December
1832, I was returned for the new and popular constituency of South Hampshire. In
my subsequent contests for that seat on the
two following general elections, in January
1835 and August 1837, I was unsuccessful;
but I was shortly after returned to Parlia-

ment for the borough of Portsmouth, upon
the vacancy occasioned by the decease of
John B. Carter, Esq., in February 1838,
and I still sit for that Borough (in January
1852), having been re-elected at the last
general election in August 1841, so that I
have now sat in Parliament altogether for
about *eighteen years :* the first *eight* for close
boroughs, and the last *sixteen* for popular
constituencies.

The attendance and associations of a Parliamentary life were, in the first instance, and,
I may say, for some years, highly gratifying
to me, even under the disadvantage of sitting
for a close borough. To hear matters of the
highest and most momentous interest dis-
cussed night after night by the most splendid
orators of the age, and especially the illustrious Canning, in the meridian of his glory,
was an intellectual feast, not likely soon to
pall upon the appetite. The opportunity also
which my attendance in Parliament gave me
to extend my acquaintance with public men,

and generally with men eminent for their
merits and talents, in all the higher walks
of life, was extremely interesting and pleasant,
and I readily concurred in opinion with those
who pronounced the House of Commons to
be (though rather an expensive one) the best
club in London!

Gradually, however, I became less con-
tented with my position. I began to say to
myself, with the Roman poet, "Semper audi-
tor tantum, nunquamne reponam?" Still,
never having had any practice in public
speaking, I had not self-confidence sufficient
to enable me to break the ice without the
stimulus of necessity, and *this* stimulus was
never presented to a member for a close
borough. I had no constituents for whom
it might have been both my *right* and my
duty to plead, and I, therefore, naturally
shrank from the ordeal of a first address to
so awful an assembly, when I had no other
plea than that of my own powers to amuse
or instruct, for occupying its attention. I had
literally *nothing to do*, and, therefore, I hope it

will not be a very serious charge against me, that I *did nothing!* I gave, like many others, many a silent, and, I trust, honest and conscientious vote; and it is possible that the public service would not have suffered very materially if *some* of those members whose harangues now occupy so many columns of our newspapers during the Parliamentary season, were to follow my example!

When I was first returned for a popular constituency I was in my fifty-second year, and it was already far too late for me to enter upon the career of a regular Parliamentary debater with any chance of success; but whenever circumstances, or my peculiar position in the House, have called me forth, I trust I have not been wanting, and, in point of fact, I have addressed the House of Commons *forty-nine* times during this *second* stage of my Parliamentary life. I must gratefully acknowledge that I have on all such occasions received from the House both courtesy and encouragement.

There is another defect in the position

of a member for a close borough, of which
I soon became deeply sensible, and which
it appears to me impossible for any ingenuous
mind to contemplate without some degree of
humiliation and pain, and which consequently
appears to me very much to strengthen the
argument for the abolition of those boroughs.
I felt that I entered the House under *false
colours!* I felt that I was *not* what I professed
to be, really the representative of the borough
for which I was nominally returned. I came
into Parliament by means which, under the
circumstances of the case, I conceived to be
perfectly justifiable, but which, being *illegal,*
I could not rise up publicly in my place and
avow. It may have been useful and right
that a certain number of seats in Parliament
should be attainable by *purchase,* or through
the *influence of certain wealthy commoners or
peers ;* but I consider the false position in
which members for close boroughs were
placed in the House, under the old system,
wholly indefensible, and that these boroughs
were, therefore, very properly abolished.

It is alleged that the representatives of open boroughs and counties often owe their seats in the House of Commons to means equally indefensible. It may be so. But this, when it is so, is a matter of choice, not of necessity. Few election contests have been more severe than those which I have encountered, once successfully, and twice unsuccessfully, in South Hampshire, and my expenses amounted upon the whole to some thousand pounds; but these were perfectly legitimate expenses, the accounts of which might have been laid upon the table of the House of Commons, and every item of which I could have boldly stood up in my place in the House to avow and to defend. I can solemnly declare that, to the best of my knowledge and belief, not a shilling was expended on my behalf, either in the purchase of a vote, or in any corrupt transaction of any kind, for the purpose of procuring my return! I contend, therefore, that, when a candidate now resorts to underhand means of obtaining a seat in Parliament, the fault is *not* in the system, but *in himself*.

At the period of the passing of the Reform Bill my social position in the country had become somewhat different from what it had been when I first came into Parliament for a close borough. Instead of being, as it were, a stranger, just landed from China, I had become, by the purchase of a respectable property and residence, near Havant, in Hampshire, in some degree a country gentleman, and known in person or in character to the electors in that part of the country. When, therefore, the disfranchisement of all the close boroughs had closed the doors against me at Heytesbury, and had opened them more widely for popular constituencies, by the increase to the number of county members, I resolved upon offering myself for South Hampshire. I stood upon perfectly free and independent principles, and I was for some time the only avowed candidate.

Still, it was perfectly obvious that I had no
chance of success, unless one or other of the
two great political parties espoused my cause.
When, at length, the former Tory member,
Mr. Fleming, was brought forward by his
friends, the Liberal party determined to op-
pose him with two candidates, whom they
supposed favourable to their views ; and they
accordingly addressed a special requisition to
Lord Palmerston and myself to come forward
in the Reform interest. My principles as a
moderate and constitutional reformer were
well known. I had voted against the Duke
of Wellington on the Civil List, and for the
second reading of the Reform Bill : but, on
the other hand, I had supported the motion
of General Gascoigne, which had been considered adverse to the Bill, and I had
declined voting either for Lord Ebrington's
motion of confidence in the Whig ministry,
or even for the Reform Bill itself on the
third reading. The independent *middle* course
which I had thus indicated by my votes was
further explained by me to the electors in

public addresses. I was, therefore, fully entitled to consider their subsequent requisition and offers of support as made to me *upon my own terms.* I accepted, of course, the offer, and so did Lord Palmerston; we immediately handed over to the Reform Committee, in equal shares, a sufficient sum to meet the ordinary legal expenses of an election. This proceeding was denounced by the opposite party as a *coalition,* which, if it meant merely a *union of interest* for a specific object, was perfectly *true;* but in the sense in which it was imputed, of a *sacrifice of principle,* and of individual independence, was no less grossly false. I was perfectly *astounded* by the virulence of the invectives with which I was assailed in hand-bills, and 'in all the country papers in the adverse interest. Even a shilling pamphlet was printed and published in London, entitled "A Letter to Sir Geo. Staunton, Bart., on his Pretensions to the Representation of South Hants, and the Means by which they are Promoted!" I have had, in the course of my life, perhaps more than my share of *public praise*, but this accumulation of *public censure* on my devoted head was certainly quite new to me. I was perfectly aware that great license is usually taken at contested elections, but the outrageous violence and scurrility of the attacks upon me exceeded anything that I had imagined possible. The object of these attacks was, no doubt, to intimidate me, and, if possible, to prevent me from appearing on the hustings; but they were, I think, eventually rather of service to me than otherwise, as they roused within me a spirit, for the vindication of my personal honour, which the mere question of the loss or gain of an election would not have excited. I replied, in the first place, to the charges made against me, as far as they appeared to deserve it, in counter-addresses and handbills, and, when the day of nomination arrived, I publicly announced from the hustings that I was ready to meet *personally* every charge, and to answer every question that could be put to me. Although the Southampton populace were, on that day, mostly in the interest of

my competitor (as appeared by the show of
hands), my speech was cheered; and not a
single question was put to me. The polling
took place on the 18th and 19th of December, 1832, and I was returned by what, under
all the circumstances, may justly be termed
a triumphant majority, the numbers having
been,—Fleming, 1276; Staunton, 1530; Palmerston, 1625.

One amongst the calumnious reports
against me, which had been circulated
during the contest, drew from my assem-
bled friends and neighbours in Hampshire
the following reply in my vindication, which
is too flattering and gratifying to me not to
be here inserted:—

" *To the Editor of the Portsmouth Herald.*
" Sir,
    "Having seen in your report of the pro-
ceedings of the meetings of the electors of Portsmouth, &c., on Thursday, the 13th instant, an
observation reflecting on the *popularity of Sir
George Staunton*, stated to have been made by
Mr. Hector, wherein he is reported to have said,

'He had been informed that Sir George was by no means popular in his own neighbourhood,' we, the undersigned, feel ourselves imperatively called upon, in justice to so highly respectable an individual, to express our surprise at such an uncalled-for and erroneous imputation, and thus publicly to assert, from our own knowledge and experience, that the conduct of Sir George has been uniformly unimpeachable, as a neighbour and a gentleman, and that his general urbanity of manners, liberality, and benevolence, have rendered him universally popular in this neighbourhood, and fully entitle him to this testimony of our esteem and regard.

" *Havant, September* 17*th*, 1832.

(Signed)

SAM. CLARKE.	JOHN A. OMMANNEY.
HEN. J. LEEKE.	SAM. GLOYNE.
CHAS. SHORT.	JAS. ROBINS.
JAMES HEWETT.	CHAS. CHARGE.
NEWMAN COOTE.	JOHN BALBECK.
JAS. NORRIS.	GEO. A. SHAWE.
JOHN LELLYETT.	CHRIST. STEVENS.
G. R. MOUNTAIN.	CHAS. E. ANDREWS.
G. D. RENAUD.	RICHARD GUBBINS.
THOS. GAWNE.	S. J. ALDER.
CHAS. OSBORN.	CHAS. B. LANGCROFT.
S. POYNTZ.	

In justice to the late Mr. Hector, it is right to add that he immediately retracted the statement which he had erroneously made; and was, from that time, always on the most friendly terms with me.

Nothing could exceed the triumph and exultation of the popular party in South Hampshire on the success of this election. The triumphal entry of the cavalcade of myself and friends into Havant, and our subsequent procession to Emsworth, and back, after the election was over, and our success announced, will long be remembered in the neighbourhood.

The part I took in Chinese affairs during the two years that I sat for South Hampshire, by moving Resolutions, and supporting a uniform rate of Tea duties, has been already stated. I also spoke shortly on the Navy estimates, Agricultural distress, the Malt-tax, Observance of the Sabbath, Dissenters' grievances, and Emsworth fisheries; but I felt a peculiar pleasure in having had an opportunity of rising in my place and vindicating my friend and late colleague in China, Mr. Ellis, against a vexatious attack that had been made upon his pension. This drew from him and his brother-in-law, the Earl of Ripon, the following notes of acknowledgment:—

"*Pell Office, Saturday.*

"My dear Sir George,

"Your kindness last night must ever add to the many reasons that I have long had for feeling towards you the most sincere regard and attachment. Pray accept my most sincere thanks for the friendly part that you have taken ; and believe me, when I say, that the testimony borne by an individual holding the place in public estimation that you do, was highly valuable, and produced a considerable effect in the House.

"Believe me, most truly yours,
(Signed) "H. ELLIS.
"Sir George Staunton, Bart."

"*Putney Heath, March* 15th, 1834.

"My dear Sir George,

"I cannot resist the impulse which urges me to express to you my sincere and grateful thanks for the very generous and handsome testimony you bore, in the debate last night, to

K

the character and services of our friend, Henry
Ellis. You had ample opportunity of seeing what
was in him, and of appreciating his capacity for
public employment : and allow me to add, that
the independence of your own character and station in the eye of the public, could not but give
the greatest additional weight to your testimony
in his favour, and mainly contributed to the triumphant result of the discussion, which was intended, as I firmly believe, to have effected his
degradation, if not ruin, as a public man.

"I shall ever feel grateful to you for your
kindness upon an occasion in which, for many
reasons, I took the liveliest interest ; and remain,
my dear Sir George, with real regard,

"Very sincerely yours,

(Signed)   "RIPON.

"Sir George Staunton, Bart."

Everything went on smoothly during the
sessions of 1833 and 1834, and I was wholly
unprepared to expect the catastrophe which
took place at the end of the latter year. I
really begun to give credit to the sanguine
aspirations of my friends, that I was now
seated for South Hampshire for life. My
assiduity in attendance on the House, and

my regularity and courtesy in corresponding
with my constituents, were praised by *both*
parties. The moderation and independence
of my votes and conduct seemed also generally admitted. I appeared to have lost no
friends, and to have gained over some adversaries, and, in short, to be gaining favour and
popularity every hour. I little dreamed that,
while I was absent upon an excursion to
Paris, in the autumn of 1834, an event would
take place which would, in its consequences,
rob me of the fruit of all these golden opinions.
Earl Spencer having died, Lord Melbourne
was dismissed, Sir Robert Peel sent for. The
stream of ministerial influence became adverse;
a dissolution of Parliament followed. All
my personal claims were forgotten, and my
boasted majority of 254, in 1832, was, in
1835, converted into a minority of 209. Mr.
Fleming and Mr. Compton were chosen to
represent South Hampshire, instead of Lord
Palmerston and Sir George Staunton.

In the midst of all the mortification of
this defeat I had several sources of conso-

lation. As my noble colleague, notwithstanding his rank, great talents, and influence, was rejected, as well as myself, it was evidently a mere *political*, and not a personal defeat. Even Mr. Fleming, whose committee had so much abused me in the course of the contest, acknowledged in his public address, upon his election, that his opponent was "an honourable and worthy Baronet, highly esteemed in private life, and supported by a large body of influential and active friends." In spite of the adverse current of ministerial influence, I had a decided majority in the Portsmouth and Fareham districts, in which I was best known, and which, in fact, formed about one-half of the southern division of the county. Had, therefore, the polling for candidates been so adjusted that each quarter of the county should return one member, instead of each half returning two members, I should have still retained my seat. In my own immediate neighbourhood, that is to say, within the ten parishes nearest to my residence, at Leigh Park, the favourable feeling towards me was still more decided, and I had a majority over my opponents of four or five to one. Lastly, the actual number of voters who polled for me was 1474, that is, 198 more than my *now* victorious opponent had polled when I defeated him.

It was said by the Tories that I might have succeeded had I *stood alone.* At that time neutrality was wholly out of the question. *Standing alone* could mean nothing else than *going over to the other side!* Such a desertion from the camp of the Reformers would, undoubtedly, have paralysed their exertions, and given Mr. Fleming an easy victory, without putting him to the trouble or expense of finding a fourth candidate. But no plausibilities could have varnished over the disgrace of success obtained through such pretensions of independence.

I received the following letter from Lord Palmerston, shortly after our defeat :—

" *Broadlands, 22d January,* 1835.

" Dear Staunton,

" If such an address as you have drawn up

were expedient, nothing could be better than that
which you have framed ; the argument founded on
a review of the poll is conclusive, and your allusion
to the future is to the point. But I own I think
we had better ' let *ill* alone.' It is not, I believe,
an invariable practice for defeated candidates to
address the electors, and none of our friends have
as yet suggested anything of the kind to me. Is
it not more dignified to say nothing, than to put
forth that which, word it as we may, might be
misrepresented as the language of complaint, or
as empty boastings as to what we mean to do (as
our adversaries would say) seven years hence ?

"Talleyrand used to say that, on some occasions,
il n'y a rien de si éloquent que le silence: and, in
our present position, perhaps it is the best line to
take. To address without announcing a positive
intention to stand again would look like a resignation ; while to declare now our positive intention
of standing again, would only afford our opponents
a fair pretence for commencing immediately measures of organisation, which might add to our
difficulties hereafter. When you have nothing
to say (runs the proverb) say nothing ; and I
doubt whether we have anything to say on the
present occasion which can be much worth saying.
We *could*, indeed, say many things which our
adversaries would not like to hear, if we were at

liberty to vent in an address our secret thoughts ; but, as we cannot say all we think, perhaps it may be as well to hold our peace.

" I am perfectly convinced that, after another registration, we should win easy. It is possible that, upon the present registry, with a change of Government and a dissolution, we might succeed, especially if the price of wheat were to rise a little. I am sure the distress of the farmers, and their inability to pay rent and tithes, may be classed amongst the main causes of our defeat ; the squire and the parson never had before so great a pull upon the rustic voter.

" Yours sincerely,
(Signed) " PALMERSTON.
" Sir George Staunton, Bart."

In consequence of the death of King William the Fourth, Parliament was dissolved, and another general election succeeded as early as August 1837. During this interval I never relinquished the hope of having an opportunity of regaining my lost position in the county, but I, unfortunately, on one occasion, put a serious obstacle in the way of my own views, by the following advertisement, which, however honest and candid, I must now confess, was not dictated by a sound discretion.

" *To the Electors of South Hants.*

" Gentlemen,

" I understand that some of the electors are desirous of knowing my sentiments on the Irish Church Appropriation Clause.

" On this subject I have no hesitation in stating that, although I cordially concur with His Majesty's present Government upon most points, I cannot support them upon this or any other question which involves in it an alienation of church property to secular purposes.

" These are no new sentiments of mine. I acted upon them in Parliament, when I supported Lord Althorp against the motion of Mr. Ward. I distinctly declared them, at a very numerous and highly respectable meeting of my supporters, at Fareham, on the 9th of December, 1834, and they were at that time received, apparently, with unanimous and unqualified approbation.

" I feel confident, therefore, that this renewed declaration of my sentiments upon this subject will not separate me from any of those friends with whom I have hitherto had the happiness of acting, and who generously supported me through two arduous contests. But, be that as

it may, I would scorn to owe the vote of any
elector to a misconception of my views upon a
matter of so much importance.

  "I have the honour to be, gentlemen,
    " Your most faithful servant,
      (Signed)   " GEO. THOS. STAUNTON.
" *Devonshire Street, March* 16*th*, 1837."

This advertisement, apparently so moderate and inoffensive, immediately drew down
upon me a torrent of abuse from the Radical
paper of Southampton, and, as my leading
friends of the Reform party refused to come
forward with any counter-statement in my
vindication, I withdrew from my position
as a candidate in disgust, and announced
my retirement by advertisement.

This breach with the Reform party was
afterwards healed when they found no more
thorough-going candidate would step forward, and the course which they adopted
was to address to me a requisition to stand
in conjunction with my friend and former
proposer, the late Admiral Sir John Om-
manny. The professed object of this junction

was to secure the second votes, and, thereby, to strengthen my interest. Whether this was a wise measure or not I cannot undertake to say, but as the Admiral had neither a large property nor local influence in the county, he could not be expected to bring me any direct accession of strength, and, as his interest in the contest was professedly to be placed in subordination to mine, it was not proposed to him to take any share in the expense.

We were not successful, but we certainly fought a good fight, the numbers at the close of the poll being as follows:—

STAUNTON.	OMMANNY.	FLEMING.	COMPTON.
2080	1962	2388	2371

In this, as in the former contest, in 1835, I had a large majority in the south-east division of the county, and nearly the same preponderance in my own neighbourhood, although the increased bitterness of party rancour added a few to the number of deserters.

All prospect of my having again an op-

portunity of entering into parliamentary life
seemed now closed : but, a few months after,
in February 1838, I had the gratification of
receiving a deputation from Portsmouth, in-
viting me to offer myself for the vacancy
in the representation of that borough, occasioned by the decease of their late respected
member, Mr. Bonham Carter. This very
flattering and unsolicited invitation I certainly owe to the promptitude of my personal friends, in bringing my name forward,
and the spontaneous cordiality with which
it was at once received by the popular party.
A general feeling seemed to prevail that the
great sacrifices I had just made, personal
and pecuniary, for the Liberal cause, in the
contest for South Hampshire, gave me paramount claims over every other candidate.
The Whig Government observed throughout,
a cold neutrality, which gave rise to a suspicion that they would have been better
pleased had the popular choice in the borough fallen on a candidate who was less
independent, and more of a partisan. When,

however, it became apparent that the contest must practically ensue between the Tory candidate, Dr. Quarrier, and myself, the Government, of course, gave me its support. There was, indeed, for a short time, a third candidate, in the person of Sir Charles Napier, who, if he had persevered, would have divided the Liberal party, and, though he had no chance of success himself, would have very much narrowed my majority, if not absolutely transferred it to Dr. Quarrier. The retirement of Sir Charles Napier was soon followed by that of Dr. Quarrier, who, however, appeared at the hustings, when I was returned without further opposition. I do not know that I have much right to complain of the coldness of the Whigs upon this occasion. I was for a long time opposed to them, and when I became, in conjunction with the liberal section of the Tories, a supporter of their ministry, I was on all occasions studious to show that I did so on principle, not on party grounds, and that I looked to the measures rather than to the men. On the other hand, I think they might have recollected that such independent and conscientious support, though not so sure and uniform as that of the partisan, is, when it is given, the most valuable of any; that I had given them, with entire absence of any interested motive, many such a vote, and had made great sacrifices for the cause, without ever having drawn directly or indirectly on their patronage for my own private interests, or those of any of my personal friends.

My position in Parliament for so important a borough as that of Portsmouth was little, if anything, inferior to that which I had previously occupied as the representative of the southern division of the county, and was more suited to my habits, which, although I always spent a portion of my summers in the country, could hardly be considered those of an ordinary English country gentleman, since I was neither a farmer, nor a sportsman, nor a magistrate; and, in fact, not very often seen beyond the precincts of my library or my garden!

My popularity with my new constituents, whom I have now served for twelve years, and who re-elected me in 1841 and 1847, without opposition, is, I am willing to flatter myself, undiminished; but, in the year 1839, next after that in which I was first elected, the most inveterate and persevering efforts were made for about three months continuously to deprive me of this popularity, and to render my re-election impossible, by the same Radical Southampton paper which had previously attacked me with so much virulence in 1837. The basis of these attacks was my vote against the *ballot*, after my falsely alleged pledge to support it, and my vote against one of the clauses of the Education Grant (though I had supported the Grant itself), by which I was charged with having endangered the safety of the Ministry. As these attacks were enforced with considerable shrewdness and ability, it was a great trial of patience to wait until a suitable opportunity for refuting these charges should arrive. This opportunity was happily afforded me

on the 16th of October of the same year,
at a great public dinner given at Portsmouth, on the occasion of Mr. Baring's
re-election for Portsmouth as Chancellor
of the Exchequer, when my explanations,
given in the presence of the very author
of the calumnies, the editor of the paper,
were received with unanimous satisfaction
and hearty applause.

I have seldom been called upon to speak
in Parliament, since my election for Portsmouth except in reference to China; but I
spoke, in 1839, shortly in vindication of my
friend, Sir John Barrow, and on the question
of the Ballot, and the Education Committee;
and, in 1843, I seconded Mr. Baring's motion
for papers relating to the removal of Mr.
Hoskins from his office of Deputy Judge
Advocate of the Fleet, and I spoke in favour
of the Bill for the Suppression of Dog-carts.

My re-election for Portsmouth, in 1841,
without an opposition, or even a dissenting
voice, was peculiarly gratifying to me, after
the sinister prophecies of the Southampton

paper already alluded to; and, after I had discovered that a discontented individual of the Liberal party had been secretly using his endeavours to prevail on a gentleman of considerable wealth and influence in London, who had been before in Parliament, to come forward on more extensive and radical principles of reform, for the purpose of supplanting me.

The change of the ministry, in 1841, considerably lightened the duties of my station, as member for Portsmouth. Under the Whig ministry, although I strictly forbore to ask for anything, either for myself or for my friends, I always considered it a part of my duty to submit the claims and applications of any of my constituents, that came before me, to the favourable consideration of the department of the Government which they concerned; but, from the time that I occupied a seat on the Opposition benches, any reference to any of the officers of Government upon matters of patronage became, of course, out of the question. I say "Opposition benches," because, of actual practical opposition there has been very little on my part. The moderate con- stitutional reformers in the House, are, at present (1845), amongst Sir Robert Peel's most ordinary supporters, and are generally well satisfied with his measures, as carrying out the principles of reform quite as far as the circumstances of the country and the state of parties will warrant, and much farther, in point of fact, than is within the competency of his opponents.

In May 1843 great excitement was felt on the subject of the Factory Children Edu- cation Bill, especially amongst the Dissenters; and my colleague, Mr. Baring, and I attended a meeting at Portsmouth, on the subject, on which occasion our speeches were very well received, and our votes in Parliament against the Bill, which was ultimately withdrawn, being in perfect unison with the wishes of our constituents, were very popular.

In the same manner, on the 18th of De- cember, 1845, during the temporary suspension of Sir Robert Peel's ministry, a meeting took place at Portsmouth, upon the all-engrossing question of the Corn-Laws, which I felt it necessary to attend, although the ministerial negotiations necessarily detained my colleague, Mr. Baring, in town. I was most cordially received, and got through my speech with, I think, more than usual success. The League newspaper of the 27th of December, states that " the meeting was addressed by Sir George Staunton, the respected member for the borough, in a speech of great power and earnestness, in which he scouted the very notion of compromise."

In order to counteract any report that might have been circulated, that I did not intend to stand again for the borough, I took the opportunity of assuring the electors, that, although the last session of Parliament had been a very laborious one, and I had at one time entertained doubts how far I might continue to feel adequate to perform adequately the duty of representing them, I thought no man ought to shrink from his post at this crisis from any consideration of personal convenience to himself, and that, consequently, I should be happy to continue to devote my best services to their cause, as long as I had the happiness of enjoying their confidence. [In point of fact, I did not finally retire from Parliament till July 1852.]

Since my last return from China I have devoted a portion of every year to excursions and travels in England, Ireland, or the Continent.

My travels in England it is not worth while to dwell on. My only visit to Ireland was in the year 1828, but, in the course of that short visit, I made arrangements upon my patrimonial property which will be of great advantage and importance both to my tenants and to my successor. I then gave instruction for the rebuilding of the mansion in a style suitable to the extent and character of the estate; and I have since made to my cousin, Mr. Lynch, who inhabits it, such allowances as enable him to discharge the

duties of a resident landlord, in the same
manner as if he were the actual proprietor.
I have thus no obligation of duty to lead
me to revisit that country; and I must confess that its disturbed and agitated state in
1846, and until very recently, has hitherto
discouraged me from doing so for the mere
object of relaxation and amusement. I am
not, however, without hope of being able to
go over to Ireland in the course of the ensuing summer, for the purpose of having
the pleasure of personally inspecting, [as I
did in that year, 1846,] the improvements
that have been effected.

The following account appears of my
Irish property in my friend, Mr. Barrow's,
Account of his Tour through Ireland, in
1834 :—

"The situation of Clydagh is admirable. It
possesses all the attractions that wood, water, and
mountain scenery, can contribute to make a residence agreeable. It is embosomed in a dense
wood, partly of young growth, and from the
windows is a beautiful view of Loch Corrib, to

the borders of which the grounds descend with a gentle declivity. The house of Clydagh is surrounded by about one hundred and eighty English acres of wood, sixty of which are of younger growth. The underwood is almost exclusively composed of hollies, which grow naturally in the greatest abundance, and afford the finest cover for game, every variety of which abounds on the eastern shore of Loch Corrib. I was told that forty-two couples of woodcocks were shot in one day in the wood of Clydagh, in November last. Clydagh is only three miles from the town of Headford, where there is a good market and a daily post.

" Though the dwelling-house, in which Mr. Lynch resides, is called Clydagh, the name of the estate is *Cargin*, so called from one of those numerous old castles, now in ruins, which are generally found standing on slight eminences, overlooking a great extent of country.

" This estate is under the excellent management of Mr. Lynch, who, being a near relative, takes so great an interest in all that concerns it, that Sir George can scarcely be deemed an absentee. The property consists of between eleven and twelve hundred English acres. They are of excellent quality, partly arable and partly pasturable. On this property there are three large farms, held by opulent graziers residing thereon; and a considerable part is let to an industrious and respectable class of peasantry, who reside also on their respective little farms, not exceeding from ten to twenty acres each. On every farm is built, by the proprietor, a neat and comfortable dwelling, with some detached offices ; and in front of each house flowers and shrubs are planted, indicating the comfort of the tenant and the fostering care of the landlord."—P. 249-253.

I extract with pleasure the following recent confirmation of Mr. Barrow's favourable report of the condition of my Irish tenantry, from the printed Report of the Tuam Agricultural Society, for 1843 :—

" The improvements in the cleanliness, order, and general appearance of the cottages of the small farmers, are very apparent; and we beg leave to instance those on the estate of Sir George Staunton, at Clydagh, as the most striking. In that district there is scarcely a house that does not merit a premium."

The above report does great credit to my cousin, Mr. Lynch's, management, and is a convincing proof that the Irish peasantry are not that unimproveable race that has sometimes been alleged, but that they will readily respond to sincere and strenuously-pursued measures for their benefit and amendment.

I will now proceed to give a short notice of my several tours on the Continent. I have always been disposed to condemn those who, without necessity or some adequate cause, have domesticated themselves for considerable periods in foreign countries, and have thus placed themselves and their children in a position to acquire an undue taste for foreign habits and usages, which they may find it very difficult afterwards to unlearn, when afterwards settling finally in their native country. But, foreign travel, when not comprising a longer residence at the remarkable spots visited than may be requisite for the formation of a thorough acquaintance with the interesting objects they contain, appears to me not only to enlarge the mind, and enrich it with new ideas, but to

be rather calculated to strengthen our natural
affections for home than to weaken them, to
augment our patriotism rather than to diminish it. I know, at least with respect to
its influence upon my own feelings, that,
however much I have been gratified by the
various sights which I have witnessed on
the continent of Europe, I have hailed no
object with a sincerer pleasure than the first
view of Dover Castle from the sea, upon
my return!

My first excursion to the Continent was
in the autumn of 1818. I left London on
the 27th of June, and returned to it on the
12th of November. My course was, first,
to Paris, where I spent three weeks, then
to Geneva, and, after making the tour of
Switzerland, and visiting Chamouny, across
the Simplon into Italy as far as Milan. From
thence I proceeded direct to Venice, and
returned by the Tyrol, and the banks of the
Rhine, to England, resting a few days on the
route, at Munich, Aix-la-Chapelle, and Brussels. I was accompanied from Paris, as far

as Aix-la-Chapelle, by Mr. Hayne, my former associate in Lord Amherst's Embassy. He was obliged to hurry on to England from thence alone, on account of private business. A great portion of this route I have since repeated, but there is always a peculiar interest and freshness in first impressions. The journey, however, somehow or other, did not agree with me, for I was for a short time, a few days after my return, seriously indisposed. This illness probably discouraged me, for I did not visit the Continent again till 1823.

My second visit was a very short one, and only to Paris. I left London on the 30th of May, and returned on the 18th of June. It was on this occasion that I was first presented to His Majesty, Louis Philippe, then Duke of Orleans, and I had the honour of dining with His Royal Highness at Neuilly. My recollections of this short visit to Paris are, however, embittered by its connexion with the deep affliction which I sustained by the death of my mother, during my absence. Her health had been for some

time declining, but no immediate danger
had been apprehended, and I returned home
upon the first summons, on a change for the
worse, but she had ceased to live two days
previous to my arrival! I was thus fated to
be absent at the moment of the decease of
both of my dear and affectionate parents.
My grief was bitter, and not soon assuaged.
I had the mournful satisfaction of attending
the funeral in person, and have placed a suitable tablet to her memory on the walls of
Marylebone Church, where she was interred.
My father having been buried in Westminster
Abbey, I had previously erected a monument
to his memory there, in the form of a sarco-
phagus, with bas-reliefs, ably executed by
Chantrey. The virtues of both my parents
are also commemorated on the pedestal of
a cenotaph urn in the Temple of Friendship,
in the gardens at Leigh Park.

The interesting ceremonials and entertainments on the occasion of the coronation
of Charles X., drew me a third time to
Paris, in 1825; and, after remaining there

between three and four weeks, I extended my tour into the south of France, visiting, in the course of my route, Orleans, Tours, Bourdeaux, Bagnères on the Pyrenees, Montpellier, Marseilles, Toulon, Nismes, and Avignon, thence to Nice, and across the Col de Tenda to Turin; and from Turin back again across the Alps by the Mont Cenis, to Chamberry and Geneva; and, finally, by way of Paris, to England. I was absent altogether from England, from the 27th of May to the 9th of September. This visit to Paris was peculiarly interesting to me. The extent and splendour of the fêtes and assemblies far exceeded anything of the kind to which we are accustomed in England. In 1818 I had been introduced to, and had dined with, the Counts *La Place* and *Bertholet*, the Countess Rumford, and some others distinguished in the walks of science and literature. On the present occasion I saw a good deal of Talleyrand, Soult, and other political leaders, and also the different branches of the Royal Family. My visit to the south of France, during the heats of July and August, was rather ill-timed, on account of the great heat, and I suffered a good deal in consequence, but I was, on the whole, much gratified and interested.

Upon this occasion I travelled *alone*, which, upon a balance of conflicting considerations, I am inclined to pronounce the preferable plan, unless with a person united by ties of family affection, or very happily coinciding in views, temper, and constitutional powers, and tastes.

My fourth excursion on the Continent, in 1826 and 1827, was the longest and most important of any that I have made, and would have proved still more agreeable if circumstances had permitted me to have devoted an entire twelvemonths to what was rather hurried over in seven or eight months. I left town on the 20th of September, and returned on the 9th of May, of the following year. My namesake and relative, Dr. Staunton, of Longbridge, joined me at Paris, and accompanied me throughout the rest of the journey. We proceeded by the Jura road to Geneva, thence across the Simplon to Milan, Genoa, Florence, Rome, and Naples : then back from Naples, to Rome, and through Ancona, Bologna, Parma, Venice, and the mountains of Carinthia, to Vienna, finally returning home by way of Munich, Frankfort, and Brussels. We not only saw the chief objects of curiosity which this interesting route presented to us, but had the honour of audiences of the Pope, the King of Naples, and the King of Bavaria, and of dining with the Grand Duke of Tuscany, the Archduchess of Parma (widow of Napoleon), the Queen Dowager of Wurtemburg, and the Landgravine of Hesse Hongburg. I may also boast of the still rarer honour of dancing (that is, walking the Polonaise), at the ball at Parma, with the Archduchess, the ex-Empress of France!

I happened luckily to have been at Parma during the season of the entertainments of the Carnival, and no Englishman of higher rank than myself being present, I received honours, to which, under ordinary circumstances, I certainly could not have aspired. I was not only placed next to Her Majesty (for that was the title the Archduchess assumed) at the dinner-table, but one of the Royal boxes at Opera was allotted to my exclusive use, during the week of my stay. When, in reply to an inquiry respecting my route, I said I was going to Venice, which, I lamented, was rather in decay, the Archduchess retorted with quickness, " It is very true, but I assure you my father cannot help it!" However that may be, I was pleased to see, on a subsequent visit, in 1843, some appearance of bustle and improvement, so that I trust that the imputation of the Austrian government having sacrificed Venice in order to promote Trieste, is unfounded.

I also received much attention from the Grand Duke Leopold of Tuscany, at Florence. Besides being invited to the Royal dinners and balls, I had several private audiences, and, on taking leave, received from the Grand Duke's own hands a magnificent copy of the works of Lorenzo de Medici. This last compliment was probably conferred on me in consequence of my having translated for him a Chinese inscription in the Royal Museum. I also gave the librarian my opinion in writing of a Map of Marco Polo in the library; and, some years after, I was much surprised and amused to meet with this opinion of mine in print, and quoted, in the original English, in a note to a recent edition of the works of Marco Polo, by the Count Bandelli.

My fifth visit to the Continent was a short excursion to Paris, in January 1829. Although the winter was remarkably severe, I spent a few weeks at Paris very agreeably. I saw Charles X. open the Chambers with great state, amidst loud acclamations, little anticipating that the abrupt close of his reign was so near at hand. I also dined with the celebrated Cuvier, and was introduced to several other French *savans*.

I had long wished to see Holland and the North of Germany, and accordingly devoted about a couple of months to this object,

in company with my excellent friend, the late
Mr. Guillemard, in the summer of 1830. I
set out on this, my *sixth* tour, on the 21st
of May, and returned the 17th of July.
Commencing with Calais, for the sake of
a short sea passage, we proceeded by Antwerp
to the Hague, Leyden, Haarlem, Amsterdam,
and Utrecht, in Holland, and Cassel, Göttingen, Leipsic, and Dresden, in Germany. In
the course of our return we visited Toplitz,
Carlsbad, Frankfort, and the Rhine. We
saw the veteran Blumenbach at Göttingen,
and were hospitably entertained by Mr. Guillemard's friends, at Dresden, Toplitz, and
Carlsbad, the Prince Clary, Count Caraman,
and others; and I only regret that the intelligence of the death of George IV., and
the necessity of an immediate return to England, with a view to a seat in the new parliament, prevented me from visiting Prague,
[which, however, I did in 1852.]

My seventh visit to the Continent, in
1834, has been already alluded to, as having
occurred at the memorable period of the

abrupt dismissal of the Melbourne ministry, and recall of Sir Robert Peel. I was absent from England from the 23d of October till the 1st of December, and had the honour of being received at the Tuileries, and dining with King Leopold at Brussels, but my excursion was not otherwise remarkable.

I paid another short visit of a few weeks to Paris, in November 1838, in which nothing very remarkable occurred except that I had the honour of dining with the King at the Tuileries, and renewing my acquaintance with the distinguished traveller, the Baron Humboldt. I had also an opportunity of testing the extraordinary proficiency in the Chinese language and literature of Professor Julien, who has formed a regular Chinese school at Paris, and put to shame our total neglect of the Chinese language and literature in London, until that stigma was happily removed, some years after, by the appointment of a Chinese Professorship in King's College, in 1850.

After this journey I had in great measure

renounced the idea of further Continental travelling, until 1841, when, having the comfort and convenience of a more confidential servant to attend upon me than I had on previous occasions, I was encouraged to venture on another attempt; and I have now made five more autumnal journeys in five successive years, with considerable profit and pleasure; although I cannot but feel that the naturally increasing delicacy and uncertainty of my health, as I advance in years, increase the risks and diminish the advantages of such excursions.

My excursion in 1841 was limited to a visit to Brussels and Paris, making the circuit of the Ardennes to see the city and Cathedral of Rheims. I partook, as formerly, of the amusements of these two capitals, and had the honour of audiences of the two monarchs, Leopold and Louis Philippe; but the greatest novelty to me was my first experience of a railway journey between Brussels and Antwerp. I have since travelled some thousand miles by this new and strange conveyance;

the most wonderful and influential of the discoveries of the present age, but I shall always remember the sensations of anxious surprise and curiosity with which I performed my first journey.

My excursion on the Continent in the autumn of 1842 was more adventurous than that of the preceding year, and was extended as far as Munich. On this occasion I, for the first time, ascended the majestic Rhine in a steamer, and I have more than once repeated that delightful navigation with undiminished pleasure. In the course of the journey from Frankfort I visited the interesting cities of Wurtzburg, Nuremburg, and Ratisbon, and the beautiful Classic Temple of the Walhalla, recently erected by the King of Bavaria on a commanding situation on the banks of the Danube. At Munich I could not feel otherwise than delighted with the splendid exhibitions it affords of ancient and modern art. The grand galleries of painting and sculpture, and the beautiful frescoes and stained glass with which the present sove-

reign has adorned his capital, are famed all
over Europe. Still, Munich is badly paved
and lighted, and has no good market. Is not
our Brighton or Cheltenham, which have
been contemptuously described as unmeaning
aggregates of houses, but which possess these
advantages, more truly indicative of genuine
civilisation! I had the gratification of witnessing the ceremony of the opening of the
petty Parliament of Bavaria by the King, in
one of the most magnificent saloons in Europe; and could not but be struck with the
contrast of our own Parliament, which may be
said to rule the destinies of the world, and
was, till lately, opened by our Queen, in a long,
narrow, inconvenient room, into which not
one-tenth of the Commons of England, who
are supposed, and have a right to be present,
could, by any possibility, have been admitted.
On my return I stopped a couple of days
at Stuttgart, and was honoured by a very
gracious audience of the King of Wurtemburg.

In the autumn of 1843 I made an excursion of ten weeks into the north of Italy,

as far as Venice and Genoa. The weather
was very favourable, and I hardly remember
a more delightful fortnight than that which
was occupied in travelling from London to
Milan. The majestic Rhine was already
familiar to me, but the picturesque graces
of Baden-baden, the impressive grandeur of
the falls of the Rhine, the stupendous scenery
of the Via Mala, and Pass of the Splugen,
and, finally, the softer beauties and lovely
repose of the Lake of Como, cannot easily
be forgotten. I say nothing here of Venice,
Genoa, Turin, and Geneva, because they had
been already well known to me; and I was so
satiated with Paris, on this my tenth visit to
that capital, that I did not even once revisit
the gallery of the Louvre. I was, however,
gratified by receiving an invitation to dine with
the King at St. Cloud, and was honoured
with the same gracious notice from His
Majesty and the Queen that they had con-
descended to show me more than once on
former occasions.

I took the opportunity of the autumn of

1844 to supply an omission in my former tour in the north of Germany, in 1830; and visited Hanover and Berlin, so that I may now boast of having seen all the most important cities of Germany, with the exception of Prague and Hamburg; which, indeed, I have also since visited in the year 1850.

Hanover was not very interesting, except as the original seat of our Royal family, and did not detain me long; but I spent a fortnight very agreeably in the magnificent city of Berlin. The pleasure of this visit was very much enhanced by the kind and unremitting attentions of my venerable friend, the illustrious traveller, Baron Humboldt, whose introduction procured for me the most gracious notice from the King and Queen, and the honour of dining with them, first at the summer residence at Potsdam, and, afterwards, at the royal palace in Berlin. I should here also notice, as an evidence of the general courtesy of the German character, and their accommodating spirit to strangers, that I was enabled, in this and the preceding year, to travel into the heart of the country with a mere smattering of the language on *my* part, with perfect ignorance of it on the part of my servant, and without any courier.

Two notes which the Baron Humboldt addressed to me while at Berlin, are so characteristic that I am tempted to insert them :—

"Le Roi et la Reine, vous ne saurez douter, auront le plus grand plaisir de recevoir Sir George Staunton à Sans Souci. Un nom, illustre comme le votre, inspire toujours le plus vif intérêt. Ayez la grace, monsieur, d'annoncer votre arrivée par deux lignes à M. le Maréchal de la Cour, Baron de Mezeray, à Potsdam. Ecrivez simplement que, restant peu de jours à Berlin, vous désirez faire la cour au Roi. Le Directeur des Musées, M. D'Olfers, a la plus grande envie de vous offrir ses respects et de vous guider à Berlin. Mille tendres hommages.

(Signed)   "A. HUMBOLDT."

"Mons. le Baron,

"Je suis si triste de ne pas vous voir, mon respectable ami, que. rentrant demain, lundi matin, avec le Roi en ville, j'ose vous demander la grace de me recevoir chez vous, à votre Hôtel de St.

Petersbourg, demain à midi. Vous me direz alors, combien de jours nous aurons encore le bonheur de vous posséder ici, puisque le Roi m'a semblé avoir un vif désir de vous inviter encore un fois, avant votre départ, à dîner, sur notre Historique (mais aujourd'hui un peu glaciale) Colline de *Sans Souci*. Veuillez bien, Sir George, m'attendre demain lundi chez vous, à midi, et agréez l'hommage renouvellé de ma haute et affectueuse considération.

(Signed) " A. HUMBOLDT.

" *à Potsdam, ce dimanche matin.*"

My Continental excursion of the last autumn was shorter, less interesting in its destination, and less enjoyed, on account of my health having been indifferent, than any of four preceding ones. Still, in the course of four weeks, I was amused with the sight of several interesting objects at Ghent, Brussels, Bonn, Coblentz, and Mayence, and the interesting Roman antiquities at Treves; and the romantic town of Luxembourg, and the remarkable cities of Metz, Verdun, and Chalons, which I saw on my return through the north of France, were entire novelties.

Having now completed a brief notice of
my travels, my Parliamentary life, and my
literary engagements, it remains for me to
say something of my social position.

One of my first objects upon finally
settling at home, was to discover an eligible
opportunity of investing a portion of my
property, not exceeding a moiety, in the
purchase of a country residence and estate.
I was well aware of the inexpediency of
allowing myself to be seduced by the *éclat*
of a large estate to invest my entire property
in that manner; and was sensible of the truth
of the adage, that he whose resources are
exclusively his acres, however many, will
always be *poor*, that is to say, will, whatever his nominal income, be embarrassed
by, and unprepared to meet, extraordinary
pecuniary emergencies. But, subject to this
proviso, I was most desirous to have what
is called "a stake in the hedge," although
I knew it must be attended with very great
sacrifice of income, and that it would oblige
me to be content with a more modest town

residence than those of the more opulent of my own class and rank in society: this did not much signify to me as a bachelor, for whom a very large house was not required, and hardly becoming. A respectable country residence and estate, I felt, would give me, (what no man can possess if confined to the metropolis,) a sphere of action peculiarly my own, which, when suitably taken advantage of, would be calculated to extend and improve my social position, and proportionably add to my happiness.

I think I have been peculiarly fortunate in my selection. The Leigh Park Estate is of a size suited to my means, at an easy day's journey from London, and half-way between the popular watering-place of Brighton and Salisbury, the place of my birth, and the residence of the greater portion of my maternal relations. The situation is healthy; the views, including that of the sea, are beautiful; and, although the mansion is of a modest size, and the park not large, the character of the property has been much

raised by the addition of a handsome Gothic
library, by the construction of numerous
hot-houses and conservatories, famed for the
successful cultivation of rare flowers and ex-
otic fruits, and by the very great extension
of the pleasure-grounds, generally admired
for their picturesque views and various
decorations.

The society of the neighbourhood consists
mainly of retired officers of the Navy, gentry
of moderate income, and resident clergy; and
its tone is unquestionably much better suited
to my habits and character than that which
is met with amongst the great sporting and
agricultural proprietors, the old, original,
country gentlemen of Yorkshire and Dorset-
shire. I have always received from my
neighbours in Hampshire, with very rare
exceptions, and, notwithstanding the shock
and excitement of political conflict, great
kindness and courtesy, of which I have
already recorded a notable instance, in the
very handsome testimonial in my favour

which they addressed to the public papers at the period of my first election contest.

Amongst these neighbours, and with as large a selection of my relatives and friends as my accommodation would admit, in the character of guests under my roof, I have generally spent about three months at Leigh Park in each succeeding summer; and have had as much enjoyment in the possession of that social retreat as the imperfection of all human contrivances for the promotion of comfort and happiness, can ever be expected to permit.

My social position in London has been, of course, of a more exciting and mixed character, and my residence there, seldom less than six or seven months every year, much longer. Besides the regular avocations of Parliament, I have received pleasure and profit from an occasional attendance at the meetings of the numerous literary and scientific societies of this great city, in which I am enrolled; and I have partaken, in due subordination however to the consideration of my health and habits, of a sprinkling of what are called the gaieties and amusements of London, but I have never mixed much either in the very aristocratic or very fashionable world. The circle of friends and acquaintances whom I have either inherited or formed in the course of my life, consists, for the most part, of persons of my own class and rank, or not materially above or below it, and is extensive and pleasant to the full extent of my wishes.

The only one of the great public institutions of London in which I have taken practically and regularly an active part, is the Royal Asiatic Society, founded by the distinguished Orientalist, Mr. Colebrooke, in the spring of 1823. I was invited to cooperate with him on its original formation, and I have ever since held the office of one of its Vice-presidents. To assist in founding their library I presented to them my whole collection of Chinese works, in about three thousand small volumes, and also about two hundred European works upon China, and some articles of curiosity for their Museum.

I record with pleasure the following letter from my friend, the late Right Hon. Sir Gore Ouseley, as giving an interesting testimony to my early exertions in aid of this Society:—

"*Woolmers, Hertford, February* 21*st*, 1823.

"Many thanks, my dear Sir George, for your obliging favour of yesterday, and its enclosure. I have long thought that an institution similar to that which has now emanated from Mr. Colebrooke and your Committee, in the luminous prospectus you have had the goodness to send me, was a desideratum of the greatest importance; and I accept with great thankfulness your obliging offer of subscribing my name in the list of original members, and of communicating the same to the Committee.

"My brother, Sir William, lives entirely at Crickhowel, near Abergavenny, and, consequently, could not well be a resident subscriber, but I should think he would be proud of becoming a non-resident one. Believe me, my dear Sir George,

"With great truth, most sincerely yours,

(Signed) "GORE OUSELEY.

"Sir George Staunton, Bart."

One of the most flattering literary compliments I ever received, was, certainly, the following dedication to me by that elegant and distinguished scholar, the late Mr. Charles Butler, of his publication entitled "Reminiscences:"

To Sir George T. Staunton, Bart., LL.D., F.R.S.

"Sir,

"One of the earliest and most pleasing reminiscences of my literary life is my acquaintance with your father. When we were both young his various learning and elegant accomplishments attracted my attention and reverence; his long political career, ever marked by honour, integrity, talent, and beneficence, was beheld by his numerous friends with delight and respect, and in these feelings, and the joy of seeing all his great and good qualities revived in his son, no one participated more than myself. It is pleasing to me to have this opportunity of recording the friendship with which he and yourself have so long honoured me. With the greatest regard, I have the honour to be,

"Your obliged and obedient servant,

(Signed) "CHARLES BUTLER.

"*Lincoln's Inn, 28th February,* 1822."

I have already stated that I was chosen a
Fellow of the Royal Society, and a member
of Dr. Johnson's celebrated Club, at a very
early period, soon after I became of age.

In 1818 the University of Oxford con-
ferred upon me the honorary degree of
Doctor of Laws. I have since been chosen
Foreign or Honorary Secretary of the Royal
Academy, a Parliamentary Trustee of the
Hunterian Collection, and a Vice-President
of the British Association of Science.

I have no other public honours to record;
but I flatter myself that those who advert to
the weight of the testimonials which I have
here registered, of the nature and amount
of my public services in Lord Amherst's
Embassy,—services which, it ought to be
remembered, were wholly gratuitous, will
think that if some mark of Royal favour
had, upon that occasion, been conferred
upon me, it would not have been unworthily bestowed. I did not, out of delicacy to Lord Amherst and Mr. Ellis, press
my claims as long as they continued un-

noticed; but, upon His Lordship's appointment to the high station of Governor-general of Bengal, and Mr. Henry Ellis to a lucrative appointment at the Cape of Good Hope, this motive for reserve ceased to exist, and I considered that it was become a duty that I owed to myself no longer to delay bringing my claim forward. I was informed privately that a Baronetcy might probably have been conferred on me, had I not already possessed that honour by inheritance, but that a seat in the *Privy Council*, the next step in the ladder of ambition, was not usually conferred in such cases as mine. Lord Liverpool wrote to me as follows:—

" I am sorry to say I do not feel that the circumstances of your case can be considered as coming within the description of those for which the honour you solicit has been usually conferred. In saying this I must at the same time beg you will do me the justice to believe that it is not from any want of disposition to do justice to your services, that I feel myself unable to forward your views."

Mr. Canning added,—

N

" Of Mr. Ellis's appointment to the Cape, indeed, I know nothing but that it was given to
him by friends interested in his individual welfare,
not in any degree as a reward, but as a provision.
As to Lord Amherst, I can say, with the most
perfect confidence, that, so far from the Embassy
to China having the slightest share in producing
his appointment to the Government-general of
India, that appointment originated very much with
myself,—I mean, on my suggestion, on grounds of
private friendship, and of an opinion of general
fitness in the person for the office, and that, if
the Embassy to China was adverted to at all,
in the course of the discussions respecting it,
the question upon that Embassy was, rather,
whether its unsatisfactory issue was a reason
against, than whether the having filled it was
a qualification *for*, his present nomination.   It
would, indeed, have been hard that a failure, in
which there was no fault, should have weighed
against so many recommendations from estimable
and amiable character ; but I can take upon myself decidedly to affirm that *reward* for the Embassy to China never entered into the mind of
any one who had a share in the choice of Lord
Amherst."

It is not difficult to find *public* reasons,

like the foregoing, for not doing that which for *private* reasons may be inconvenient; but if I had had a personal *friend* in the Cabinet, he would not have been put down by such arguments. He would still have contended that an individual who had been pronounced by the authorities in China, (who beyond all question were the most competent judges,) to have " maintained our national honour and promoted our commercial interests, by his decision and sound judgment, under circumstances the most trying, when less firm minds might have bent under the weight of the responsibility he incurred," was justly entitled to some reward. He might have further contended that this reward was doubly due to him, when those who had taken the opposite and less praiseworthy cause, and when his conduct alone had saved from actual disgrace, were, nevertheless, from whatever cause, honoured and promoted; and he would finally have scouted the idea of what had been the *usual practice* being pleaded as a bar to reward in a case so absolutely peculiar and unprecedented. When, some years after, Mr. Henry Ellis and Mr. Holt Mackenzie were made Privy Councillors; neither previous services nor usual practice were regarded. It was quite sufficient that the one was the friend of Lord Ripon, and the other of Lord Glenelg. They are both most estimable and talented individuals, but I apprehend that there can be no question that this is the true history of their promotion to that honour.

There is another ground upon which my promotion to a seat in the Privy Council might have been recommended, that of *public utility*, on the score of the expediency of having at least one member of the Privy Council locally acquainted with China, when matters connected with that country, as occasionally occurs, are brought before it; and I have been informed that it was actually in contemplation to place me in the Privy Council on that ground, when the private interests of an individual with which the proposal seemed to militate, caused it to be over-ruled.

The last time the question was brought forward was in 1837, during the short interval that occurred between my failure in the contest for South Hampshire and my election for Portsmouth.

The moment that I was replaced in Parliament, and that any application, even for a just reward, might be construed into solicitation for personal favours, and compromise my independence, I withdrew my request, and cancelled the application.

Lord Melbourne wrote me the following complimentary letter :—

"*Windsor Castle, August* 31*st,* 1837.

"Sir,

"I beg leave to acquaint you that I received your letter of the 29th, here, and, at the same time, to acknowledge most unequivocally the great service which you have rendered to the Government by coming forward as a candidate for South Hants, and the claims which such conduct gives you to every mark of consideration and respect. I very much lament that your efforts have been unsuccessful, but the failure is in no respect to be attributed to any want of zeal, energy, or exertion, on your part.

"I can only assure you that I appreciate the force of all you have urged, the firmness of your principles, and the extent of your sacrifices, and that I should be most happy to find myself able to give any mark of my high opinion that it was in my power consistently with other considerations to bestow."

"*Windsor Castle, September 4th.*

"With respect to your present request, I am sure you will forgive me for observing that the Privy Council has lately been increased and extended to an unprecedented degree, and that the introduction of every new name produces an additional number of new claims. You ground yourself upon the cases of Mr. Henry Ellis and Mr. Holt Mackenzie, and others would immediately find, in your being sworn in, a reason for their receiving a similar mark of Royal favour. You will, I am sure, feel the necessity of some limits being drawn, and will therefore not be surprised if, whilst I solicit your services and claims, I request to be allowed some further time for consideration before I undertake to bring your application before Her Majesty.

"I remain, &c., &c.,
(Signed) "MELBOURNE.
"Sir Geo. Staunton, Bart."

I trust it will not be considered that I have done anything derogatory to my position and character in thus urging my claims from time to time, whenever I thought a suitable opportunity offered. I have done no more than every naval and military officer who conceives he has achieved anything worthy of reward does, and is considered fully entitled and justified in doing, on any similar occasion. It would, certainly, have been very pleasant to me to have received this mark of Royal favour within a reasonable time after the return of the Embassy of Lord Amherst to England, while my mother, who would have been so much gratified by witnessing it, was alive, and while I was myself still young enough to form and hope to realise fresh projects of ambition; but the prefix of " Right Honourable " to my name would add little indeed at present to my happiness, or even to my character and position in society. If there were nothing else to disentangle me from the pursuit of such vanities, my age and valetudinary state of health are sufficient. It will be much more becoming in me to devote for the future my chief thoughts to the highest and most important of all objects, the considerations of religion. I gratefully recollect the manner in which one of my earliest preceptors, of the name of *Mackay*, directed the thoughts of my childhood to God. The religious books which I took out with me to China when a youth were my own seeking and purchasing. I have, at all times of my life, as far as I have had the opportunity, taken the part of the religious world against their adversaries. Since I have settled at home I have become a pecuniary contributor to many religious Societies, and in some few cases have taken the chair at their meetings. I am not so absurd as to record these things as a boast, and am sensible, on the contrary, that the higher I rate my religious professions, the more humiliating will be the inferiority of my religious practice. All I contend for is, that we must not lower our professions to the standard of our practice, but strenuously endeavour to raise our practice to the standard of our professions. I confess, also, that I do not understand the religious principles of those who are bitterly severe upon everything they conceive to be *religious error*, but very placable and indulgent in cases of *no religion at all!* —who can rail at " Popery," and yet permit pretended scientific treatises, teeming with Atheism and Infidelity, to appear on their tables! I hold that the *poor Indian*, who bows to his idol, and thus, in his rude way, acknowledges that there exists a power above us to which we are accountable, is nearer the kingdom of God than the *modern philosopher* who derives the universe and everything in it from an unreflecting first cause, a *Primordial necessity!* I cannot express my creed in this matter better than in the sublime language of Burke in his Reflections on the French Revolution:—

" We know, and, what is better, we feel inwardly, that *religion* is the basis of civil society, and the source of all good and of all comfort.

We are so convinced of this, that there is no rust of superstition, with which the accumulated absurdity of the human mind might have crusted it over in the course of ages, which we do not prefer to *impiety*.

"Violently condemning neither the *Greek*, nor the *Roman* church, we prefer the *Protestant*, not because we think it has *less* of the Christian religion in it, but because, in our judgment, it has *more*. We are *Protestants*, not from indifference, but from zeal."

GEORGE T. STAUNTON.

Devonshire St., London,
January 19th, 1846.

LIFE OF GIBBON.

In applying to my own case the following passages extracted from Mr. Gibbon's autobiography, I have not the remotest idea of instituting any comparison between myself and that eminent writer. I have no pretensions to the high literary reputation which he achieved, nor has my humbler reputation been stained by the grave faults which he has committed, but some of the coincidences in our respective positions and circumstances are certainly remarkable :—

" I cannot reflect without pleasure on the bounty of nature, which cast my birth in a free and civilised country, in an age of science and philosophy, in a family of honourable rank, and decently endowed with the gifts of fortune."— P. 17.

"I have never possessed or abused the insolence of health."—P. 28.

"I am tempted to enter a protest against the trite and lavish praise of the happiness of our boyish years, which is echoed with so much affectation in the world. That happiness I have never known, that time I have never regretted."—P. 31.

"In my fifteenth year (at the University) I felt myself suddenly raised from a boy to a man; the persons whom I respected as my superiors in age and academical rank, entertained me with every mark of attention and civility, and my vanity was flattered by the velvet cap and silk gown!"—P. 32.

"Every man who rises above the common level has received two educations, the first from his teachers, the second, more personal and important, from himself."—P. 60.

"Nature had not endowed me with the bold and ready eloquence which makes itself heard amidst the tumult of the Bar."—P. 80.

"I had not been endowed by art or nature with those happy gifts of confidence and address which unlock every door and every bosom."—P. 81.

"I never handled a gun, I seldom mounted a horse, and my philosophic walks were soon terminated by a shady bench, where I was long

detained by the sedentary amusement of reading
or meditation. At home I occupied a pleasant
and spacious apartment; the library, on the same
floor, was soon considered as my peculiar domain;
and I might say with truth that I was never less
alone than when by myself."—P. 83.

"My behaviour satisfied my father, who was
proud of the success, however imperfect in his
own lifetime, of my literary talents."—P. 130.

"My travels, the House of Commons, and the
fame of an author, contributed to multiply my
connexions: I was chosen a member of the
fashionable clubs."—P. 144.

The following passages do not altogether
apply to my present position in Parliament,
but they are very descriptive of the first eight
years of my Parliamentary life, while I represented a Cornish borough:—

"I was returned at the general election, and
supported with many a sincere and silent vote the
rights of my country. After a fleeting illusive
hope, prudence condemned me to acquiesce in the
humble station of a mute. I assisted at the debates
of a free assembly; I listened to the attack and
defence of eloquence and reason; I had a near

prospect of the characters, views, and passions, of the first men of the age."—P. 146.

"In the premature dissolution which followed I lost my seat. I was now delivered from the hopes and fears of political adventure; my sober mind was no longer intoxicated by the fumes of party, and I rejoiced in my escape."—P. 166.

I do not know whether Mr. Gibbon was quite sincere in the joy that he expresses at his escape, but I know, with respect to myself, that the resumption of a Parliamentary life in 1830, and afterwards in 1838, was very agreeable to me.

The following notices of Mr. Gibbon's position at Lausanne, are remarkably appropriate to mine in Hampshire:—

"In London I was lost in the crowd. I ranked with the first families (in Lausanne). Instead of a small house between a street and a stable-yard, I occupied a spacious and convenient mansion, open on the south to a beautiful and boundless horizon."—P. 166.

"Where is the spot in which I could unite the comforts and the beauties of my establishment at Lausanne!"—P. 179.

" The certainty of my tenure has allowed me
to lay out a considerable sum in improvements
and alterations ; they have been executed with
skill and taste, and few men of letters, perhaps, in
Europe are so desirably lodged as myself."—P. 180.

February 23*d*, 1846.

I conceive myself peculiarly fortunate in
my career of life. I have suffered comparatively little from *defects* which, under other
circumstances must have been fatal to me.
I have a weak and delicate frame, but, although I have travelled much by sea and
land, I have never been subjected to any
severe bodily trials. I am in many respects
unfitted to make my way in the world, but
my *way* has, in great measure, been *made
for me*. My position in China insured me
moderate wealth. My literary fame, if I
have any, was acquired in the closet. My
share in Lord Amherst's diplomacy was an
occasion which I did little to bring about,

though I trust I met it with sufficient energy and spirit.

My first eight years in Parliament was an affair of *money*. My subsequent election for *South Hampshire*, and its fruit, my present seat for *Portsmouth*, was a happy accident; and all I can claim is, that I met the crisis, which was to me a difficult one, perhaps better than might have been expected. My present advantages in respect to wealth, rank, and station, and, I trust, character, would probably have made my social position higher than it is, if I knew how to make the most of them, but, still, it is a very good one, and ought to satisfy my reasonable ambition.

G. T. S.

December 27*th*, 1846.

Since I closed this Memoir, in February last, I have, I trust, been usefully employed in my vocation, in endeavouring to raise a subscription for the endowment of a Chinese

Professorship at King's College, an institution much wanted in this country, for it is
a disgrace to England to be obliged to send
her youth to Paris or Berlin for instruction
in the Chinese language, whenever they wish
to acquire that qualification, for commercial
or other pursuits in China. Although I have
met with some difficulties and opposition, on
which I had not calculated, yet, as upwards
of two thousand pounds have been already
raised, I cannot consider myself unsuccessful.

I have also made an interesting tour to
Ireland, and I have had much gratification in
witnessing the comfortable and handsome
establishment in which I have been able
to place Mr. George Lynch, whom I may
call my adopted son, in the seat of my
Irish ancestors on the banks of Loch Corrib.

It is also very pleasant to me to be able
to record the following letter from the Earl
of Aberdeen, dated Haddo House, Dec. 9th,
1846 :—

    " My dear Sir,

       " I must thank you for the letter which you

had the goodness to send me from Sir John Davis; and I will also take this opportunity of expressing my obligations to you for the earnestness with which you pressed your opinion of his merits upon me. I can truly say that in no appointment was I ever more anxious to discover the person best qualified to fill the situation, being well aware of the great difficulties he would have to contend with.

" It may, therefore, be a satisfaction to you to know that, during my whole correspondence with Sir John Davis, I do not recollect a single circumstance in which his conduct did not meet with my full approbation ; and that I have always been strongly impressed with a sense of his great ability, judgment, and temper. That he has many detractors I know; but I sincerely hope that he will meet with the official support he so well deserves, and that his merits will ultimately be acknowledged as cordially by all as they now are by me. I am, my dear Sir,

      " Very truly yours,

        (Signed)   " ABERDEEN.

" Sir George Thos. Staunton, Bart."

APPENDIX.

I.

THE accompanying short Memoir was given in the " Penny Cyclopædia:"—

" STAUNTON, SIR GEORGE LEONARD, was the eldest and only surviving son of Colonel George Staunton, of Cargin, in the county of Galway, Ireland, a gentleman of small fortune, but descended from a very ancient English family. He was born at Cargin, on the 19th of April, 1737, and received his education partly in Galway and partly in Dublin, until he entered his sixteenth year, when the delicate state of his health, and a tendency to consumption, rendered necessary an immediate removal to a warmer climate. His father accordingly sent him to Montpelier, in the south of France, where he remained some years, and having completed his studies in the college of that city, he took a medical degree.

" In the year 1760 he returned to England, and

o 2

resided for some time in London, where he occupied himself in contributing some valuable essays to the periodical publications of that day, and formed an acquaintance with many eminent literary men of the time, especially Dr. Johnson, who, in the year 1762, upon his intended embarkation for the West Indies, wrote him a most affectionate valedictory letter. This letter is preserved in Boswell's 'Life of Dr. Johnson,' and bears a very high testimony to Mr. Staunton's merits at that early period.

" Mr. Staunton practised for a short time in the West Indies as a physician, but he held at the same time considerable official situations in the islands, and having acquired a competent fortune, which he invested in estates in the island of Granada, he returned to England in 1770. In 1771 he married Jane, the second daughter of Benjamin Collins, Esq., of Milford, near Salisbury, and a banker in that city ; but the disorder into which his West Indian property fell in his absence obliged him very soon to return to Granada, where he continued to reside until the capture of the island by the French in 1779.

" During this period Mr. Staunton devoted himself with considerable success to the practice of the law, a profession much more congenial to his talents and habits than that of medicine, and he

was appointed by the Crown Attorney-General of
the island. In 1774 Lord Macartney went out to
Granada as Governor, and a very warm intimacy
and friendship was soon formed between that no-
bleman and Mr. Staunton, which ended only with
their lives. Mr. Staunton's established influence
and character in Granada rendered his aid and
support of essential advantage to the administration of the new Governor, and these and other
services his Lordship warmly and affectionately
acknowledged.

"Upon the capture of the island by the French,
Lord Macartney and Mr. Staunton were both sent
to France as prisoners of war. Lord Macartney
immediately proceeded to England on his parole,
but Mr. Staunton remained some time longer at
Paris, and had the address and good fortune to
obtain, under circumstances of peculiar difficulty,
his Lordship's exchange, as well as his own. Lord
Macartney was thus enabled to avail himself of
the appointment which the East India Company
had conferred upon him, of the government of
Madras, and Mr. Staunton accompanied him to
India as his confidential secretary. In this character he was in fact his Lordship's chief adviser
on all the various transactions of his arduous and,
upon the whole, successful government.

" Nothing could have been apparently more
adverse to Mr. Staunton's interests than the capture of Granada. His house and plantation, which
unfortunately lay in view of the enemy when they
were landing, were totally pillaged and destroyed.
Everything moveable was, taken away, and the
land itself was afterwards in part confiscated and
given away to Frenchmen upon frivolous pretences.
The recovery of any part of the wreck of his fortune was rendered hopeless by his sudden and
compulsory departure from the island, and he was
reduced to the necessity of commencing, as it were,
the world anew.

" These circumstances, seemingly so unpropitious, were, nevertheless, in the end, of great
advantage to him, for they led to his immediate
removal to a more suitable sphere for the exercise
of his talents.

" While in India, Mr. Staunton was engaged
in a series of missions of great importance. On a
very critical occasion, when the civil and military
authorities at Madras were at issue, he undertook
the delicate and possibly hazardous office of execu-
ting an order of the government, placing under
arrest the Commander-in-chief of the army, Major-
General Stuart ; and he thus preserved, by his
vigour and promptitude, both the tranquillity of

the settlement and the supremacy of the civil government.

"But the transaction in which his diplomatic abilities were chiefly displayed was the negotiation of a treaty of peace with Tippoo Sultan, in 1784, by which the safety of our Indian possessions'was secured at a crisis of great difficulty and peril. For this service he was immediately raised to a baronetcy, and the East India Company conferred on him a pension of 500*l*. a-year for life. On his return to England he also received the degree of Honorary Doctor of Laws from the University of Oxford.

"Lord Macartney, as well as Sir George Staunton, remained at home unemployed from this time until 1792, when the determination of the Government to send a splendid embassy to the court of Pekin called them both again into active service.

"At this period, Sir George, having succeeded to his patrimonial estate by the death of his father, and having made a moderate yet sufficient addition to it by his own exertions, was little covetous of further public employment; but the novelty of this undertaking, and the very extensive sphere of public utility to which it seemed to lead, gave it a degree of interest in his mind altogether independent of its pecuniary advantages. Although the negotiations were to have been opened by Lord Macartney, it was to Sir George Staunton that the Government chiefly looked for the final and complete accomplishment of the objects of the mission, and with this view he was provided with separate credentials as minister plenipotentiary, to be acted on in the absence or after the departure of the ambassador.

" Sir George's health fell a sacrifice to his exertions upon this occasion. A few months after his return to England he was seized with an attack of paralysis, from which he never entirely recovered, and after a painful struggle of about six years, he gradually sunk into the grave. He, however, happily retained his intellectual faculties in full vigour to the last. He gave to the world a remarkable proof of this, in his published narrative of the proceedings of the Chinese embassy, a work which was not only read with great interest and avidity at the time, but is still referred to as one of the first authorities on all matters connected with China.

" Sir George died in London, on the 14th January, 1801, in the sixty-fourth year of his age, and was buried in Westminster Abbey, where an elegant monument, by the late Sir Francis Chantrey, was some years after erected to his memory. He was succeeded in his title and estates by his only son, the present Sir George Thomas Staunton, M.P. for Portsmouth."

The following notice was given of my venerable tutor, Mr. Hüttner; and a letter, written only the year before his death, shows him in full possession of his unimpaired faculties:—

"Died, on Monday, the 24th of May, at his house in Fludyer Street, Westminster, John Christian Hüttner, Esq., of the Foreign Office, at the advanced age of 82 years, and under peculiarly painful circumstances, as he was run over by a cab in the street about a fortnight before his decease, by which accident his thigh was broken; and although he appeared for some time to be doing well, the shock proved too great for his system, and he sank under an attack of apoplexy of the heart, on the evening of the 24th of this month.

"He was a very able scholar, with an active and well-stored mind, and a placid and courteous temper; which endeared him to all with whom he had any intercourse, during his long, useful, and respected life. After the usual course of studies, and taking his degree at the University of Leipsic, he was selected by Professor Beck, on the invitation of the late Sir George Staunton, to proceed to England, in the spring of 1791, to superintend the education of his only son, then a youth under ten years of age. His pupil continued under his charge until the spring of 1797, when he entered the University.

"During this interval Mr. Hüttner accompanied his pupil to China, in the memorable embassy of Lord Macartney. As most of the diplomatic documents were written at that time in Latin, Mr. Hüttner's classical abilities were frequently called into exercise, and his services specially noted in the late Sir George Staunton's official account of the embassy.

"Among the friendships which Mr. Hüttner formed in England, one of the earliest was with the first Dr. Burney, who was much interested by some curious information he had collected on the subject of Chinese Music. It is supposed to have been mainly through Dr. Burney's influence that he received from Mr. Canning, in 1807, the appointment which he continued to hold, and very efficiently to discharge, for no less than forty years, —that of Translator to the Foreign Office.

"While still at Leipsic, Mr. Hüttner published,

in October, 1788, a learned Latin Commentary,
'De Mythis Platonis;' and in 1795 his Journal
of the Chinese Embassy was printed and published
at Zurich, but without his consent, and contrary
to his wishes; and he always expressed his regret
that his indiscreet friends had thus in some degree
anticipated Sir George Staunton's official account
of the Mission. In 1808 he translated from the
Spanish into German the highly interesting and
important Appeal of Don Pedro Cevallos to the
nations of Europe, against Napoleon's invasion of
Spain, and which is supposed to have had a powerful effect in awakening the sympathies of Germany
in favour of the Spanish cause at that period. He
is also understood to have furnished, from time to
time, some valuable articles for the 'Conversations
Lexicon,' and other leading German periodicals;
and his literary reputation recommended him to
the notice of the late accomplished Grand Duke
of Saxe Weimar, for whom he acted for many
years as Literary Agent in this country.

"Mr. Hüttner was twice married, but left no
issue. His affections, however, were latterly cen-
tered on an amiable and dutiful grand-niece, who
came over to England from Germany in 1840, and
whom he had the comfort of seeing happily married,
about a twelvemonth ago, to Dr. Freund, an eminent German physician, recently settled in this
country.

"Mr. Hüttner was born of respectable parents, at Guben, in Lusatia, was a member of the German Lutheran Church, and always through life was exemplary in the discharge of his religious and moral duties. His earthly remains were deposited by the side of his second wife, in the cemetery of Kensal Green, on the 29th instant, and were followed to the grave by a select number of his attached and sorrowing friends.

"Although neither the late Sir George Staunton, his earliest patron, nor the present Sir George Staunton, his pupil, had any direct part in procuring for Mr. Hüttner the small but competent establishment which he so long enjoyed in this country, they always entertained for him the sincerest respect and regard; the former as long as he lived, and the latter down to the present moment, when he survives to deplore his loss.

S.

"*London, June 4th*, 1847."

The Letter is as follows :—

"*Foreign Office, 7th December,* 1846.

"My dear Sir George,

"'To remind,' says your card; yes, I hope I shall be able to have the honour of tasting your exquisite wines and fare; but though this is a very

common thing to you, *to me* it is an *event*. The
longer I live the more I wonder when I find myself
seated with portraits of Lord Macartney and your
father pointing to the treaty, behind me, and with
your mother and her son George, before me. Who-
ever should have predicted this to me in 1790 would
have been laughed at. I was then in a scrape and
entirely at a loss how to get out of it. There was
no visible outlet. What I could aspire to I was
shut out from by the abilities and the interest of
my fellow-students. But in '91, in February, just
when I was most desponding and wretched, there
came your father's letter, with a valuable draft!
Such an overture was unheard of, so much so that
I was thought half-crazy for accepting it. 'A
wild, silly scheme to go to London; the English
are far from courteous to foreigners; stay in your
country, or you will return soon in disgrace.'
So they augured, and some, much worse. I alone
had courage; I was borne up by a presentiment
that your father's letter breathed the 'gentleman :'
I conned it over till I knew it by heart, and every
time I was confirmed in looking on the invitation as a lucky hit, a God-send. And how has
it turned out? Why, most auspicious, much
above my deserts, and to the utmost astonishment
of my early acquaintance. Now a dinner at your
elegant table crowns all these miracles. Instead

of being cooped up in some miserable town of
Germany, I find myself seated at a brilliant table,
among the best company, quaffing half-a-dozen of
the choicest wines, and regaling on venison, vol-au-
vent, patties, and delicacies, the very name of
which makes the mouth water ; and last, not least,
opposite sits my poor niece and her husband, also
your protégés !

"When I think of this, in casting my eye on
your card of invitation, (and I think much of it,)
I cannot but thank my star that piloted me safe to
64 Berners Street. Pardon this garrulity of, my
dear Sir George,

"Yours most faithfully,

JOHN CHR. HÜTTNER.

"Sir George Staunton, Bart., M.P."

II.

"At a Meeting of the Council of King's College,
London, held on the 12th June, 1846, the Lord
Bishop of London, Chairman of the Council, in
the Chair; His Grace the Archbishop of Canter-
bury, Visitor of the College, and other Governors
and Members of the Council, being present ; the

following Proposals, which were submitted by Sir George Thomas Staunton, Bart., were unanimously adopted, and ordered to be advertised in the Public Papers.

Proposals for the Endowment of a Chinese Professorship in King's College, London.

" Our present relations with China present a vast field for British enterprise. Five of the principal ports of that empire are now open by treaty to British commerce. Our missionaries, merchants, and men of science, have already visited many places in the interior of China previously untrodden by British footsteps. Nothing seems wanting to enable British subjects to carry on the most extended and beneficial intercourse with this vast and populous empire, but the means of readily acquiring that most essential of passports — a competent knowledge of the language of the people ; means, which are already provided in almost every great capital in Europe, except the metropolis of the British empire.

" Our missionaries will thus be qualified to diffuse, amongst a population estimated at a third of the whole human race, the inestimable blessings of our pure Christianity ; our merchants will be enabled to introduce amongst these countless multitudes a knowledge of our manufactures and productions; and by more fully ascertaining what may be most acceptable in Europe, among the articles which this ingenious and industrious people have to give us in return, will be able to lay the foundation for a vast increase of that mutually beneficial commercial intercourse which already subsists between the two countries; our men of science will, lastly, be empowered to cultivate that only remaining great field of inquiry on the globe, which our enterprising travellers have not already in great measure exhausted.

"It is therefore unquestionably an object of great public concern in a religious, in a commercial, and in a scientific point of view, to provide, as soon as possible, the means by which the requisite preliminary instruction in the language and literature of China may be obtained in this metropolis, so as to enable all persons who may be about to visit that country, to qualify themselves to enter at once into the sphere of their duties and labours immediately upon their arrival. Although it may be true, that a complete and intimate acquaintance with the written character and spoken dialects of China is not likely to be attainable solely by means of instruction received in this country, it is of essential importance to the student to have the opportunity of laying the foundation, at least, of this knowledge, previously to his departure, and while he is still in possession of the leisure and the youthful capacity which studies of this description require.

"In order to carry out these views in the most effectual manner, it is proposed to raise by subscription a fund for the Endowment of a Professorship of the Chinese language in King's College, London, including a salary for the Professor, a sum for the purchase of Chinese books, the establishment of scholarships for the encouragement of students, and such other pecuniary outlays for the promotion of the study of the language and literature of China, as the Council may see expedient to authorise.

"Subscriptions on account of the Chinese Endowment Fund will be received in London by Messrs. Coutts & Co., the Messrs. Drummond, the Messrs. Hankey, Messrs. Williams, Deacon, & Co., and Messrs. Twining & Co.; at Manchester, by Sir B. Heywood & Co.; at Liverpool, by Messrs. Arthur Heywood & Co.; at Glasgow, by the Union Bank of Scotland; at Dublin, by the Bank of Ireland; at Southampton, by Joseph Toomer, Esq.; at Newbury, by Henry Godwin, Esq.; and by J. W. Cunningham, Esq., Secretary to King's College, London.

P

Subscriptions already received:—

	£.	s.	d.
His Royal Highness Prince Albert . .	100	0	0
The Honourable East India Company . .	200	0	0
His Grace the Archbishop of Canterbury .	50	0	0
The Lord Bexley	200	0	0
His Grace the Duke of Portland . . .	100	0	0
Sir George Thomas Staunton, M.P. Bart. .	105	0	0
The Lord Ashley	10	0	0
Rev. W. Wilson, D.D.	10	0	0
The Earl of Harrowby	20	0	0
Henry Godwin, Esq.	21	0	0
M. Mouldy, Esq.	21	0	0
Lord Viscount Sandon, M.P. . . .	10	0	0
Rev. Robert Heath	1	1	0
Mrs. Heath	1	1	0
Rev. G. D. St. Quentin	10	0	0
A Friend	5	0	0
Rev. F. C. Fowle	2	2	0
Samuel Ball, Esq.	20	0	0
Lord Radstock	10	0	0
Right Hon. Henry Ellis	5	0	0
Right Hon. Sir H. Pottinger, Bart. . .	5	0	0
Colonel Leake	5	0	0
Mrs. Leake	5	0	0
Emmanuel Birch, Esq.	5	0	0
Rev. Dr. Moberly	5	0	0
Rev. Frederic Bevan	20	0	0
Thomas C. Smith, Esq.	26	5	0
Benjamin Hawes, Esq. M.P.	5	0	0
Philanthropos	20	0	0
Messrs. Coutts & Co.	100	0	0

	£.	s.	d.
James Alexander, Esq.	50	0	0
James Matheson, Esq. M.P.	26	5	0
The Earl Howe	25	0	0
The Earl of Ellesmere	10	0	0
Rev. T. S. Grimshawe	2	0	0
Sir Benjamin Brodie, Bart.	21	0	0
The Lord Bishop of Winchester	25	0	0
The Lord Bishop of Lichfield	20	0	0
W. A. Hankey, Esq.	20	0	0
John Reeves, Esq.	20	0	0
Henry Pownall, Esq.	10	0	0
Sir Robert Inglis, Bart. M.P.	10	0	0
The Earl Brownlow	10	0	0
Right Hon. W. E. Gladstone	20	0	0
Sir John Barrow, Bart.	5	0	0
Right Hon. Sir A. Johnston	5	0	0
Francis H. Toone, Esq.	25	0	0
John Bullar, jun. Esq.	1	1	0
Lancelot Dent, Esq.	100	0	0
J. R. Reeves, Esq.	20	0	0
R. Wilkinson, Esq.	10	0	0
W. Dent, Esq.	5	0	0
B. Nicholls, Esq.	0	10	0
Charles J. Bevan, Esq.	10	0	0
Robert C. J. Bevan, Esq.	10	0	0
The Lord Bishop of London	50	0	0
The Earl of Dartmouth	10	0	0
The Lord Bishop of Llandaff	10	0	0
F. Roberts, Esq.	2	2	0
Rev. F. J. Blandy	2	2	0
Thomas Weeding, Esq.	10	0	0
Rev. Dr. Griffiths	5	0	0
Sir Charles Forbes, Bart.	50	0	0

	£.	s.	d.
The Dean of Peterborough	5	0	0
The Lord Bishop of St. David's	20	0	0
Rev. Dr. Ellerton	5	0	0
The Lord Bishop of Sodor and Man	10	0	0
The Marquis of Cholmondeley	10	0	0
C. R.	2	2	0
The Misses Champion	20	0	0
W. B. Brodie, Esq.	10	0	0
The Earl of Burlington	10	0	0
Sir Trayton Drake, Bart.	5	0	0
J. Bullock, Esq.	1	1	0
Henry Bingley, Esq.	10	10	0
Rev. S. F. Montgomery	1	0	0
Hon. and Rev. G. Wellesley, D.D.	5	0	0
The Viscount Chelsea	1	0	0
Capt. G. G. Wellesley, R.N.	2	0	0
J. C. Sharpe, Esq.	10	0	0
Sir George Larpent, Bart.	10	0	0
J. N. C. Plowden, Esq.	25	0	0

For some time this Institution did not make much progress; but latterly, under the auspices of the Earl of Clarendon, several scholarships have been conferred upon these students of King's College who have obtained certificates of their proficiency in the Chinese language.

III.

The following is the return sent to Parliament on the death of the late John Robert Morrison: —

" Return to an Address of the House of Commons for Copies or Extracts of all Despatches or Communications that may have been received from China, having any reference to the services or to the decease of the late John Robert Morrison.

No. 1.

" *Extract of Minutes of Proceedings of the Superintendents of British Trade in China.*

" *August* 8, 1834.

" In consequence of the vacancy made by the demise of the Rev. Dr. Morrison, the Superintendents took into consideration the appointment of a fit and proper person as his successor. The great proficiency of Mr. Morrison [son of the deceased] in the Mandarin dialect, and the long experience in the habit and custom of communicating with the Chinese at Canton, on the part of the British merchants, for whom he has acted five years, pointed him out as a fit and proper person to fill the situation, and Lord Napier gave him an acting commission accordingly."

No. 2.

" Lord Napier to Viscount Palmerston.—
(Received February 1, 1835.)

" (Extract.)·   *Canton, August* 14, 1834.

" When the world was deprived of the valuable services of the Rev. Dr. Morrison, it was somewhat fortunate that he left behind a son eminently qualified for following in the steps of his father. He commenced his studies at an early period, under the able tuition of his father ; was removed to the Anglo-Chinese College at Malacca in 1827, during which time he perfected himself in the knowledge of the Court or Mandarin dialect, combined with the study of European literature ; and in 1830 returned to his father at Canton : since which he has been in the constant practice of writing, translating, and interpreting, for the European merchants.   In 1832 and 1833 he was employed on a mission to Cochin China ; and with these advantages he presents himself a fit and proper person for filling the situation of Secretary and Interpreter."

No. 3.

" Captain Elliot to Viscount Palmerston.—
(Received September 9.)

"(Extract.) *Macao, April* 21, 1841.

"Mr. Morrison, with no more than his usual considerateness and public spirit, has consented to undertake the responsibility of the Secretary and Treasurer's duties : but, feeling that he is not able to give more than a general supervision to the whole, he requested me to let the moiety of Mr. Elmslie's salary be divided between the two senior clerks, Mr. Almada and Mr. Adam Elmslie, upon whom the additional burden of duty will chiefly fall.

"I could not consent to this proposal, but, at Mr. Morrison's solicitation, I have agreed that one-half should be equally divided between those gentlemen, and the other half added to his own salary."

No. 4.

*" Sir Henry Pottinger to the Earl of Aberdeen.—
(Received October 14.)*

" (Extract.)   *Hong Kong, July* 31, 1843.

" I consider that the invaluable services of Mr.
Morrison as Chinese Secretary, entitle him to the
highest salary assigned. to any of the Consuls."
[Viz., 1800*l.* a-year.]

No. 5.

*" Sir Henry Pottinger to the Earl of Aberdeen.—
(Received February 8, 1844.)*

" *Macao, September* 1, 1843.

" My Lord,

" It is with the most sincere and deep
regret I report to your Lordship the death, on
the 29th of last month, at this place, of the Honourable John Robert Morrison, Esquire, Member
of the Legislative and Executive Councils of Hong
Kong, Chinese Secretary to Her Majesty's Mission,
and Chief Superintendent of Trade, &c., in China,

and Officiating Colonial Secretary to the Government of Hong Kong : an event which has plunged all classes, not only of Her Majesty's subjects, but of all other foreigners, as well as the natives, high and low, of this part of China, in inexpressible and lasting sorrow.

"I inclose a copy of an official notice, announcing Mr. Morrison's decease ; and I am assured that Her Majesty's Government will most unfeignedly participate in lamenting the untimely death, at the early age of 28, of a faithful, devoted, and invaluable servant, whose loss may be most truly declared to be irreparable.

"I have, &c.,
(Signed)   " HENRY POTTINGER."

Inclosure in No. 5.

" *Official Notice by Sir Henry Pottinger.*

" *Macao, August* 29, 1843.

" Sir Henry Pottinger announces, with feelings of the deepest and most unfeigned sorrow, the demise, this morning, a few minutes after seven o'clock, of the Honourable J. R. Morrison, Esq., Member of Council, Chinese Secretary, &c., and

Officiating Colonial Secretary of the Government of Hong Kong.

"Mr. Morrison was so well known, and so truly beloved, esteemed, and respected by all who had the happiness of his acquaintance and friendship, that to attempt to pass any panegyric on his private character would be a mere waste of words; and Sir Henry Pottinger feels that his own sincere grief on this mournful event is only a type of that universal sentiment in which the memory and worth of Mr. Morrison will for ever be embalmed.

"In a public point of view, Sir Henry Pottinger considers the death of Mr. Morrison to be an irreparable national calamity, and he doubts not but as such it will be received and viewed by his Sovereign and country."

No. 6.

"*Sir Henry Pottinger to the Earl of Aberdeen.—* (*Received January* 5, 1844.)

"(Extract.)   *Hong Kong, September* 8, 1843.

"Few men have at any age the opportunity of doing so much good to their native country as Mr. Morrison has had, when, comparatively speaking, a young man."

No. 7.

" The Earl of Aberdeen to Sir Henry Pottinger.

"(Extract.) *Foreign Office, January* 3, 1844.

"I have seen, with great regret, by the accounts which arrived in this country a few days ago from China, through Calcutta, that the illness of Mr. Morrison has terminated fatally ; and although I have not yet received any despatch from you, confirming that intelligence, your latest being dated on the 25th of August, I fear there is no reason to doubt that Her Majesty's Government have to lament the loss of a public servant, whose ability and zeal have constantly entitled him to their highest approbation.

"I conclude that I shall find in your despatches which I may expect to receive in a few days, an account of the manner in which you propose to provide for the great loss which the public service has sustained by Mr. Morrison's death ; but I think it right to intimate to you, without loss of time, that although, considering Mr. Morrison's acquirements and conduct, I gladly acceded to your suggestion, that his salary as Chinese Secretary should be fixed at 1800*l.* a-year, I should consider that sum too large in the case of any other person."

IV.

The following letter, though out of place, explains Lord Palmerston's declining to stand for the county in 1837.

"*Stanhope Street, July 3d,* 1837.
" My dear Staunton,
"Thank you for your note and address. I wish you all possible success, and should have much liked to have been fighting by your side; but my Tiverton friends wished me to stay with them, and they have behaved so handsomely to me that I could not refuse to do so.
"Yours sincerely,
(Signed) "PALMERSTON.
"Sir George Staunton, Bart."

V.

In March 1852, in consequence of a numerously signed requisition of my friends in South Hampshire, I ventured once more

to offer myself to the Electors; and at an
earlier period of my life I might possibly have
succeeded: but having gained my seventieth
year, I thought that the risk of a severe
contest too great to be incurred, and finally
determined to retire; as I fully explained in
the following letters.

" *To the Electors of South Hampshire.*

" Gentlemen,
" On the 4th of February last, I announced
to the Constituency which it has been my pride to
represent for the last fourteen years, that I had
decided on retiring from public life, at the close
of the present Parliament. The Liberal cause
appeared to me to be safe at Portsmouth; and I
gladly contemplated a release, at my time of life,
from Parliamentary duties.
" But, recently, several of my friends, who
justly stand very high, both in your estimation
and in their public position, encourage me to
believe that my services may prove acceptable to
you at the present important crisis. If this opinion
should be confirmed by such an expression of your
sentiments as cannot be mistaken, I have too deep

a recollection of your former kindness towards me, to allow of any consideration of personal ease and comfort, to stand in the way of my placing at your disposal, whatever powers I may possess of serving you.

"The new Parliament will have to decide a most momentous question, namely, whether we shall continue to maintain those great and liberal principles, the judicious application of which has brought this nation to a state of prosperity and tranquillity unexampled in our history ; or whether we shall now retrace our steps, and return to that exploded system of Protection, which would be, in the end, as adverse to the real interests of the tenant farmers of this country, as it would be, confessedly, odious and injurious to the community at large, by the enhancement of the prices of all the necessaries of life.

"If it should be your pleasure to replace me in that truly honourable position which I formerly occupied of your Representative, I trust I may be able, by an honest, independent, and constitutional course in Parliament, to prove myself not altogether unworthy of your choice.

"I have the honour to be, Gentlemen,

"Your most faithful servant,

"GEO. THOS. STAUNTON.

"*Devonshire Street, March* 31*st*, 1852."

" *Carlton Gardens, June 9th*, 1852.

" My dear Staunton,

" For your own private information I have to repeat that Sloane Stanley came to me three days ago, and showed me the last return of the Tory canvass, which was 1650 promises for Compton and Cholmondeley, and 1000 for you and Brett. This result Sloane Stanley considered as decisive in favour of his friends ; but I said that as our requisition has received rather more than 1600 signatures, without counting many who have said they would vote for you and Brett, if you come to the poll, though they did not like putting their names to a requisition, I considered the result of the two canvasses to be as yet only a tie, and that neither party could reckon on success till they had got 2500 promises. I, therefore, proposed that we should communicate with each other again when matters had got further. I must say, however, that Sloane Stanley's communication seems to me to be very encouraging to us, because they have been hard at work, and ought to have got many more promises, if there are many more voters willing to go for them. The total number registered I take to be about 6000, of which, probably, 1000 or 1200 will not

come to the poll. It seems likely, therefore, that
2500 would be a winning number.

      " Yours sincerely,
         (Signed)   " PALMERSTON."

     " *Carlton Gardens*, 23*d June*, 1852.

" My dear Staunton,

     " You seem to be in a state of great acti-
vity, and I hope your exertions will be attended
with corresponding success.

     " You will do quite right to beat all your covers
and bag as much as you can within the next few
days ; and the adverse party can find no fault
with you for doing so. On the contrary, I told
Sloane Stanley on Saturday, that I had strongly
advised you to go down and canvass personally
the unascertained votes, with a view to make up
your final determination as to going to the poll or
not, and he expressed great satisfaction at your
intention to do so. Sloane Stanley, of course, is
under the impression that you will find that the
result will lead you to retire, but I trust it may
be otherwise.

     " I have also had a conversation with Bonham
Carter, and told him what the numbers were
which Sir John Mill had reported to me as having

signed the requisition, and Bonham Carter at once acknowledged that you would not be justified in going to the poll unless you could get a much larger number of promises.

> " Yours sincerely,
> (Signed) " PALMERSTON.

" It seems likely that the dissolution will not be till Thursday of next week.

" Sir George Staunton, Bart."

> " *Carlton Gardens*, 25th *June*, 1852.

" My dear Staunton,

" I received this morning your letter of yesterday, and though sorry for the circumstances which led to your decision and for the decision itself, yet I was not surprised at the result of your canvass, and I think you are perfectly right in having come to the decision which you mention.

" The fact is, that the Liberal party, though strong in the southern division of the country, is nevertheless still a minority ; and you were quite right, as soon as you had ascertained that fact to retire from a contest, which thenceforward could only be the cause of useless trouble and expense to all parties concerned.

Q

"I thought it right to let Sloane Stanley and Andrew Drummond know your intention of retiring, and I have written to each of them accordingly.

"Yours sincerely,
(Signed) "PALMERSTON.

"The next best thing to winning an election is to retire honourably from a contest in which there is no well-founded expectation of success.

"Sir George Staunton, Bart."

VI.

In March 1853, Lord Palmerston became a Member of the Royal Society, agreeably to the permission which he gave to me by the following note:—

"*Carlton Gardens, 6th March,* 1853.

"My dear Staunton,
"I am quite ashamed of not having sooner answered your letter of last month, but I have

been struggling with an avalanche of all kinds of public business.

"I shall feel proud of becoming a member of the Royal Society, if that distinguished body should think fit to elect me, and it will give me great pleasure to enter it under your auspices.

"Yours sincerely,

(Signed)   "PALMERSTON.

"Sir Geo. Staunton, Bart."

VII.

In 1850, I published a small Tract on the proper mode of rendering the word, God; which excited at the time a good deal of attention, and still excites much controversy in China. To the opinion I then gave in favour of the term *Shang-tee*, after much consideration, I still adhere.

The following are a few extracts:—

"Almost every writer of authority on China has entered, more or less, upon this topic. Du-

Q 2

halde, the first general historian of China, is very diffuse upon it, but the following extract will suffice :—' The chief object of their worship is the Supreme Being, the lord and sovereign monarch of all things, whom they adored under the name of Shang-tee, that is, Supreme Emperor, or Tien, which, with the Chinese, signifies the same thing. But did they regard this Shang-tee or Tien, who was the object of their worship, as an intelligent being, the Lord and Creator of heaven, earth, and all things ? Is it not likely that their vows and homage were addressed to the visible and material heaven, or, at least, to a celestial energy, void of understanding, inseparable from the very matter of heaven itself ? But this I shall leave to the judgment of the reader, and content myself with relating what is learnt from the classical books.' After long and numerous quotations he thus proceeds :—' It may suffice to have shown, from the authority of the canonical books, that the Chinese nation for the space of two thousand years acknowledged, reverenced, and honoured with sacrifices, a supreme being and sovereign lord of the universe, under the name of Shang-tee or Tien. Methinks it would be doing an injury to the ancient Chinese, who followed the law of nature, which they received from their fathers, to tax them with irreligion because they had not so clear and distinct a knowledge of the Deity as the Christian world have had since their time.'—Vol. i. p. 646, folio edition.

"The Abbé Grosier, in his more recent 'History of China,' takes the same view :—'The King, or canonical books of the Chinese, everywhere confirm the idea of a Supreme Being, the Creator and Preserver of all things. They mention him under the name of Tien, or heaven, Shangtien, or supreme heaven, Shang-tee, or Supreme Lord, and Whang Shang-tee, Sovereign and Supreme Lord, names corresponding to those which we use when we speak of God, the Lord, the Almighty, the Most High.' 'This Supreme Being,' say these books, 'is the principle of everything which exists, and the Father of all living.' Duhalde and Grosier are Roman Catholic authorities. Mosheim, an eminent Protestant ecclesiastical writer, in his account of the religions of China, takes substantially the same view of the subject. 'The religion of China,' he says, 'is two-fold, one as ancient as the empire itself, and in all probability introduced by its founders. The other is of much later date, and imported from India not long after the birth of our Saviour. The latter has idols, temples, sacrifices, priests, monks, festivals, and many external rites and ceremonies. The former is free from all these, and is, perhaps, the most artless and simple of all the religions that ever were taught in the world. It prescribes reverence to an invisible being, residing in the visible heaven, and distributing from thence happiness and misery amongst mankind; but it enjoins no particular worship to him, so that temples, priests, assemblies, sacrifices, and rites, are things entirely foreign to it. The emperor alone, at certain times, offers a sacrifice to this powerful being in the name of the people. The moral part of the old system is short and easy. It consists in honouring the servants of Tien, or Shang-tee (for so the Supreme Being is called), that is, the spirits presiding over the mountains, rivers, forests, and other parts of the earth, and to some duties necessary to the welfare of the public, and of every particular family. Excepting these duties, it allows great latitude to the natural inclinations and appetites of man. The latter religion—that idolatry, I mean, which was introduced by Fo, or Foe, a celebrated Indian impostor, has a considerable party amongst the populace and women, but it is only tolerated. The wise men, and those of distinction, profess the old religion, which, besides, is the religion of the State, professed, and even preached, by the Emperor himself, and protected by the laws of the Empire.' — *Mosheim's Authentic Memoirs of the Christian Church in China, Miscellaneous Pieces.*—Vol. II. p. 21.

" The most recent, and, perhaps, most impartial authority on this subject is that of our country-man, Sir John Davis, the late governor of Hong Kong. I shall quote one or two passages from his valuable ' History of the Chinese,' to show his general coincidence in opinion with the writers already referred to :—' Of Tien, or heaven, they sometimes speak as of the Supreme Being pervading the universe, and awarding moral retribution ; and it is in the same sense that the Emperor is styled ' the son of heaven.' At other times they apply the term to the visible sky only. Heaven stands at the head of their moral, as well as physical system, and most of the attributes of the Deity are referred to it.'—P. 67.

" ' The State-worship is divided into three classes: first, the Ta-sse, or great sacrifice ; secondly, the Choong-see, or medium sacrifices; and lastly, the Seao-sse, or lesser sacrifices. Under the first head are worshipped the heaven and the earth. In this manner they would seem to adore the material and visible heaven as contrasted with the earth ; but they at the same time appear to consider that there exists an animating Intelligence which presides over the world, rewarding virtue, and punishing vice. Tien and Shang-tee (the Supreme Ruler) appear always in the Shoo-king to be synonymous.'— P. 71. ' Notwith-standing the general aspect of materialism that pertains to the Chinese philosophy, it is difficult to peruse their sentiments regarding Tien (heaven) without the persuasion that they ascribe to it most of the attributes of a supreme governing Intelligence."—Vol. II. p. 75.

I now close this short memoir of the chief incidents of my life, recommending it to the kind indulgence of the Reader.

GEORGE THOMAS STAUNTON.

Devonshire Street, May 26th, 1856.

THE END.

London:—Printed by G. BARCLAY, Castle St. Leicester Sq.

For EU product safety concerns, contact us at Calle de José Abascal, 56–1°,
28003 Madrid, Spain or eugpsr@cambridge.org.

www.ingramcontent.com/pod-product-compliance
Ingram Content Group UK Ltd.
Pitfield, Milton Keynes, MK11 3LW, UK
UKHW010339140625
459647UK00010B/697